Fish & Game Cookbook

Over 150 Recipes for Venison, Rabbit, Duck, Fish, Elk, Pheasant, Squirrel, Dove

With Nutritional Information

Bonnie Scott

Copyright © 2013 Bonnie Scott

All rights reserved.

ISBN-13: 978-1484026908

TABLE OF CONTENTS

VENISON 9

- VENISON AND PEA PODS 12
- SMOTHERED VENISON CUBES 13
- QUIRKY VENISON STEW 14
- VENISON BURRITOS 15
- VENISON RAGOUT 16
- ITALIANA VENISON 18
- VENISON LOAF 19
- VENISON CABBAGE ROLLS 20
- VENISON JERKY 21
- BARBECUED DEER MEAT 22
- WILD GAME CASSEROLE 23
- DEER CHILI 24
- BREADED VENISON STEAKS 25
- HUNTER'S STEW 26
- VENISON PATTIES 27
- HOT AND SPICY VENISON 28
- WISCONSIN VENISON SAUSAGE 30
- NO WILD TASTE MEAT LOAF 31
- VENISON STEAK FROMAGE 32
- SLOW COOKER VENISON 33

ELK 35

- ROASTED ELK WITH LINGONBERRY SAUCE 40
- SILVER BOW ELK 42
- SLOW COOKER ELK ENCHILADAS 44
- GAME MEAT ITALIAN SAUSAGE 45
- HEARTY ELK CHILI 46
- BBQ ELK MEATBALLS 47
- COUNTRY ELK MEATLOAF 48

DOVE AND QUAIL 50

- QUAIL CHASSEUR 52
- DOVE OR QUAIL CASSEROLE 53
- SPICY DOVE POPPERS 54
- QUAIL IN ORANGE SAUCE 55
- GRILLED BBQ DOVE 56
- SMOTHERED DOVES 57
- MARINATED DOVES 58
- BAKED DOVE 59

DUCK 61

- Texas Barbecued Duck 64
- Duck with Raspberry Sauce 66
- Delicious Duck Fillet Casserole 67
- Duck Stew 68
- Roasted Duck 69
- Stuffed Ducks in Wine 70
- Duck and Potatoes 71
- Chesapeake Barbecued Duck 72
- Duck Gumbo 73
- Saucy Duck with Dressing 76
- Hunter's Booya 78
- Fresh Salsa-Raspberry for Baked Duck 73
- Sweet and Sour Duck 80
- Orange Wild Duck 81
- Roast Duck with Potato Dressing 82

PHEASANT 84

- Kraut Pheasant with Apple 87
- Pheasant Supreme 90
- Wild Rice and Pheasant 91
- Grilled Marinated Pheasant 92
- Fargo Pheasant Stew 93
- Baked Pheasant in Cream 94
- Braised Slow Cooker Pheasant 95
- Pheasant in Green Peppercorn Sauce 96
- Pheasant with Stuffing 97
- Pheasant Pie 98
- Pheasant in Mushroom Sauce 100
- Cheesy Pheasant Casserole 101
- Pheasant a la Silvio 102
- Pheasant Mushroom Casserole 104
- Dakota Pheasant 87

RABBIT 105

- Rabbit in Cream 109
- Hasenpfeffer (Rabbit Stew) 110
- Rabbit Pie 111
- Rabbit in Mustard Sauce 112
- Rabbit Fricasse 114
- Rabbit Casserole 115
- Baked Rabbit 116
- Barbecue Baked Rabbit 117

SQUIRREL **119**
    SOUTHERN FRIED SQUIRREL 121
    SQUIRREL FRICASSEE 122
    SQUIRREL STEW 124

MARINADES **126**
    VENISON, GEESE OR DUCK MARINADE 126
    BEST VENISON MARINADE 127
    SOY-ONION BASTING SAUCE 128
    BASIC SEASONING SALT 129

FISH **131**
    CITRUS-MARINATED FISH FILLETS 135
    BAKED WHOLE FISH WITH MUSHROOMS 136
    SOUTHERN BASS CHOWDER 138
    SEASONED FISH 140
    LEMON FISH ROLL-UPS 141
    BAKED STUFFED FISH 142
    FISH IN CREOLE SAUCE 144
    COMPANY FILLETS 146
    BAKED FILLETS OF NORTHERN PIKE 147
    EASY FISH 'N' CHIPS 148
    EASY BAKED FILLETS 149
    MIDWESTERN FISH STEW 150
    BROILED FISH WITH DIJON SAUCE 151
    FISH WITH TARRAGON BUTTER 152
    FRIED FISH 153
    BAKED FISH FILLETS 154
    FILLET ALMONDINE 155
    FISH FILLETS IN FOIL 156
    BROILED FISH FILLETS AU GRATIN 157
    WALLEYE VEGETARIAN DELIGHT 158
    FISH JAMBALAYA 160
    BAKED WALLEYE WITH ORANGE RICE STUFFING 162
    FISH-STUFFED GREEN PEPPERS 164
    FISH-STUFFED TOMATOES 165
    ORIENTAL FISH WITH SWEET AND SOUR VEGETABLES 166
    LAKE ERIE GRILL-OUT 168
    FISH HASH 169
    FRESHWATER DRUM FILLETS ITALIAN STYLE 170
    FISH BURGERS 172

TROUT 174

- FRUIT-STUFFED GRILLED TROUT 174
- OVEN-BARBECUED LAKE TROUT 176
- BAKED TROUT FILLETS 177
- BROILED TROUT KABOBS 178
- LEMON BUTTER TROUT 179
- EASY TROUT PATTIES 180
- WINE POACHED TROUT 181
- BAKED TROUT SURPRISE 182
- GRILLED RAINBOW TROUT 184
- SMOKED TROUT SPREAD 185

PERCH 187

- CHILI-BAKED FRESH PERCH 187
- CAPER BUTTER FILLETS 188
- BREADED LEMON PERCH 189
- PERCH-STUFFED BAKED POTATOES 190
- FILLETS WITH CHEESE SAUCE 192
- BAKED FILLETS IN SOUR CREAM 193
- YELLOW PERCH WITH MUSHROOM SAUCE 194
- YELLOW PERCH BURGERS 196
- OVEN FRIED PERCH FILLETS 198
- BAKED CATFISH WITH RICE 200
- FISH CREOLE 201
- CATFISH STEW 202
- BLACKENED CATFISH 204
- STUFFED CATFISH 206

SAUCES AND COATINGS 208

- HOLLANDAISE SAUCE FOR FISH 208
- TARTAR SAUCE 209
- GARLIC SAUCE FOR FRIED FISH 210
- REMOULADE SAUCE 211
- BASTING SAUCE FOR FISH 212
- GREEN SAUCE FOR FISH 213
- RASPBERRY ZINFANDEL BUTTER 214
- SESAME MARINADE 215
- ALMOND BUTTER 216
- BEER BATTER FOR FISH 217
- LEMON BUTTER 218
- WHITE WINE AND GARLIC 219
- HERBED BUTTER 220
- BACON AND GREEN ONION 221

    Shake and Bake for Fish 222
    Cheese Stuffing 223
    Garden Stuffing 224

SIDE DISHES FOR FISH AND GAME 226

    Pineapple Salad 226
    Wild Rice Casserole 227
    Spinach and Orange Salad 228
    Cauliflower Patties 229
    Apricot Salad 230
    Southern Spoon Bread 231
    California Vegetables 232
    German Potato Salad 233
    Ever-Ready Coleslaw 234
    Fresh Spinach Salad 235
    Rice Casserole 236
    Carrot Casserole 237
    Cheesy Hash Brown Potatoes 238

VENISON RECIPES

Venison

Tips for Cooking Venison

Venison is a very low fat meat, and it's great for meat lovers who need to watch their fat and cholesterol consumption. Venison only has 170 calories in each four ounce serving and has less than 3 grams of fat. It's also a significant source of protein and provides 33 grams of protein in that same four ounce serving. Compare that with an average of 230 calories in a 4 ounce beef ribeye, along with 10 grams of fat and you'll wonder why you haven't been eating venison all along.

Aging Venison

If you've come home with a young deer that's only a yearling, there isn't any need to age the meat. It's ready to prepare as soon as you get your gear unpacked and the mud off the truck. However, mature deer need aging. Aging improves the flavor and tenderness of the meat and can be done by hanging in a cool, dry enclosure or in a spare refrigerator.

When aging meat, the temperature should be between 32 and 40 degrees Fahrenheit. The meat should be dry and protected from insects and moisture. Moist meat that is stored in temperatures over 40 degrees Fahrenheit can develop bacteria.

Marinating Venison

Marinating venison helps to remove the gamey taste that mature meat may have. Marinating in vinegar or buttermilk is very effective at removing much of the strong taste.

Large pieces of meat can be marinated for 24 hours in the refrigerator. However, don't let the meat sit longer than that, as the meat will become mushy with too much time in the marinade.

Smaller pieces of meat like steaks and kabobs should be marinated for 30 minutes to two hours.

There are many ingredients you can use for marinating venison, and you can always vary the ingredients to suit your family's tastes and preferences.

Tomato based products make good, quick marinades. Tomato juice, tomato sauce or tomato soup are good acidic marinades that help remove the gamey flavor of venison and tenderize the meat.

French or Italian dressings are ready straight from your refrigerator or pantry for no-time-to-prepare marinades.

Marinate venison in fruit juices like white grape juice, lemon, pineapple or a blend of flavors.

A basic marinade of two parts each vinegar and water and one-quarter part sugar is about as simple as it gets for a quick marinade.

Herbs and spices like bay leaves, cloves, allspice, oregano, thyme, juniper berries and nutmeg are all popular flavors to add to a basic recipe. Vegetables such as onions, garlic, celery and carrots are used as well. Soy and Worcestershire sauces, as well as wine and flavored vinegars, are all common additions to marinade recipes.

General Cooking Tips

The type of preparation you choose for cooking often depends on the cut of meat available. Dry heat, such as grilling, pan frying, roasting and broiling is best reserved for prime cuts of meat. Use loins, rump and back straps for this type of cooking. Use moist heat recipes like stews and meatloaf, or slow cooking recipes for the less tender cuts of meat.

For dry heat recipes, only cook the flesh until it is rare or medium rare. Further cooking will toughen and dry out this lean meat.

If you're grilling venison, don't take your eyes off the little devils. Venison can cook in almost half the time of a comparable piece of beef, so just stand there with your fork or spatula in hand. No wandering off for a quick potty break or to get a fresh drink.

Venison is a sweeter meat than pork or beef, so be conservative when adding sweet ingredients in your recipes until you've tried it out a time or two.

Roasting Times for Venison

To keep your meat moist and flavorful, rub the entire piece with bacon drippings or oil. Season the meat with your spices of choice and place on the roasting rack. For extra flavor and moisture, place strips of bacon on top of the roast.

Roast the meat in an uncovered pan for 20 to 25 minutes per pound at 325 degrees Fahrenheit. Insert a meat thermometer to check for doneness.

Rare: 130 degrees Fahrenheit to 135 degrees Fahrenheit

Medium Rare: 135 degrees Fahrenheit to 140 degrees Fahrenheit

Medium: 140 degrees Fahrenheit to 145 degrees Fahrenheit

Medium Well: 150 degrees Fahrenheit to 155 degrees Fahrenheit

Well Done: *155 degrees Fahrenheit to 160 degrees Fahrenheit*

Venison and Pea Pods

1 1/2 lbs. venison
2 tablespoons vegetable oil
1/4 cup soy sauce
1/2 cup water
1/4 teaspoon ginger
1 can water chestnuts (5 oz.)
1 bag frozen pea pods (16 oz.)
2 tablespoons cornstarch
2 tablespoons water

Cut the venison into bite size pieces. In an electric frying pan, brown venison in oil. Add soy sauce, water, and ginger. Cover and simmer 1 1/2 to 2 hours, stirring occasionally. Add drained water chestnuts. Dissolve cornstarch in 2 tablespoons water and add. Ten minutes before serving, add pea pods. Yield: 4 servings.

Nutrition Facts

Serving Size 375 g

Amount Per Serving

Calories 370	Calories from Fat 80
	% Daily Value*
Total Fat 8.9g	14%
Saturated Fat 1.4g	7%
Cholesterol 0mg	0%
Sodium 909mg	38%
Total Carbohydrates 25.8g	9%
Dietary Fiber 3.1g	12%
Sugars 4.8g	
Protein 42.4g	

Vitamin A 25%	•	Vitamin C 129%
Calcium 6%	•	Iron 18%

Nutrition Grade A-
* Based on a 2000 calorie diet

Smothered Venison Cubes

3 lbs. boneless venison
1/2 cup flour
1/4 teaspoon salt
1/8 teaspoon pepper
1/2 cup margarine
1 cup celery, sliced
2 medium onions, quartered
1 1/2 teaspoons paprika
2 cups chicken stock
2 cups sour cream
6 cups cooked white rice

Cut the venison into one inch pieces. Dredge the venison in flour seasoned with salt and pepper. Melt the margarine in a Dutch oven, add the venison, and brown on all sides. Add the celery, onions, and 1 teaspoon of the paprika and stir for 1 minute. Stir in the chicken stock. Cover and simmer gently for 1 hour. Stir in the sour cream and heat through, but do not boil. Sprinkle with the remaining paprika. Serve over cooked rice. Yield: 6 servings.

Nutrition Facts

Serving Size 518 g

Amount Per Serving

Calories 887	Calories from Fat 353
	% Daily Value*
Total Fat 39.2g	**60%**
Saturated Fat 15.5g	**78%**
Cholesterol 288mg	**96%**
Sodium 712mg	**30%**
Total Carbohydrates 52.9g	**18%**
Dietary Fiber 2.0g	**8%**
Sugars 2.4g	
Protein 76.3g	
Vitamin A 31%	Vitamin C 7%
Calcium 15%	Iron 72%

Nutrition Grade B+

* Based on a 2000 calorie diet

Quirky Venison Stew

2 lbs. venison
1 1/2 cups French dressing
2 carrots
3 stalks celery
1 large onion
1 small green pepper
1/4 cup quick-cooking tapioca
1 can whole tomatoes, mashed (16 oz.)
1 bay leaf
1/8 teaspoon salt
1/8 teaspoon pepper
1 whole clove

Cut the venison into one inch cubes. Place the venison in a bowl, add French dressing and marinate for 12 to 24 hours. Remove the venison from the French dressing and place the meat in a slow cooker. Pare the carrots, then cut the carrots and celery into 1 inch pieces. Coarsely chop the onion and seeded green pepper. Add the cut vegetables to the slow cooker; stir in remaining ingredients. Cover slow cooker and cook on low setting for 8 to 10 hours. Yield: 6 servings.

Nutrition Facts

Serving Size 364 g

Amount Per Serving

Calories 373	Calories from Fat 95
	% Daily Value*
Total Fat 10.5g	16%
Saturated Fat 0.8g	4%
Trans Fat 0.0g	
Cholesterol 0mg	0%
Sodium 96mg	4%
Total Carbohydrates 32.7g	11%
Dietary Fiber 3.1g	12%
Sugars 23.2g	
Protein 35.0g	
Vitamin A 89%	Vitamin C 38%
Calcium 3%	Iron 6%

Nutrition Grade B

* Based on a 2000 calorie diet

Venison Burritos

1 1/2 lbs. boneless venison round steak
1 jar salsa (16 oz.)
1 can black beans (15 oz.)
1 can Mexicorn, drained (15.25 oz.)
1 pkg. cream cheese (3 oz.)
8 8" flour tortillas
1 pkg. Mexican cheese blend, shredded (8 oz.)

Put the venison steaks in a slow cooker; cover with salsa. Using only half of the liquid from the black beans, pour the beans and liquid into slow cooker. Add the Mexicorn. Cook on low for 6 to 8 hours until the meat is fork-tender.

Shred the steak into bite-size pieces. Cut the cream cheese up into a few pieces, then stir in cream cheese until melted. To serve: Add the meat mixture to the center of a tortilla, sprinkle cheese on top and roll the tortilla up. Yield: 4 servings.

Nutrition Facts

Serving Size 678 g

Amount Per Serving

Calories 1,006	Calories from Fat 278
	% Daily Value*
Total Fat 30.9g	47%
Saturated Fat 14.4g	72%
Trans Fat 0.0g	
Cholesterol 203mg	68%
Sodium 2441mg	102%
Total Carbohydrates 101.7g	34%
Dietary Fiber 8.1g	32%
Sugars 11.3g	
Protein 87.5g	

Vitamin A 20%	•	Vitamin C 13%
Calcium 81%	•	Iron 69%

Nutrition Grade B-
* Based on a 2000 calorie diet

Note: The jar of salsa has a high sodium content. Try making your own salsa to bring down the sodium content of this recipe.

Venison Ragout

4 lbs. venison shoulder, cut into 2 inch chunks

Marinade:

1 cup cider vinegar
2 cups dry red wine
8 peppercorns
4 cloves
1 large bay leaf
1 1/2 teaspoons salt
1/2 teaspoon rosemary, crushed
1/4 teaspoon thyme

Cut:

4 medium onions, quartered
4 medium carrots, cut into chunks

Cooking Ingredients:

1/2 cup vegetable oil
1 cup dry red wine
4 beef bouillon cubes and 1 quart hot water
Additional hot water if needed
3 tablespoons flour

Combine all marinade ingredients. Place venison in large non-metallic bowl and add most of the marinade. Put onions and carrots in a large Ziploc bag and add the rest of the marinade. Cover and refrigerate at least 24 hours, turning meat occasionally so all pieces are exposed to marinade. For preparation, remove venison from marinade and pat dry with paper towels. Remove vegetables from bag. Discard all marinade.

Heat vegetable oil in stew pot and quickly brown venison over high heat. Add red wine, bouillon cubes dissolved in hot water, and the marinated onions and carrots. Add additional hot water to cover, if needed. Heat to just short of boiling. Reduce heat; cover and simmer until meat is tender, about 1 1/2 hours. Transfer venison to heated serving dish. Skim fat from pot liquids and stir in flour to thicken gravy, if desired. Pour gravy over meat and serve. Yield: 6 servings.

Nutrition Facts

Serving Size 601 g

Amount Per Serving

Calories 911	Calories from Fat 275

	% Daily Value*
Total Fat 30.5g	47%
Saturated Fat 9.6g	48%
Trans Fat 0.0g	
Cholesterol 342mg	114%
Sodium 1185mg	49%
Total Carbohydrates 18.0g	6%
Dietary Fiber 2.5g	10%
Sugars 6.5g	
Protein 111.8g	

Vitamin A 136%	•	Vitamin C 13%
Calcium 6%	•	Iron 90%

Nutrition Grade B-

* Based on a 2000 calorie diet

Note: Use low sodium bouillon cubes to bring down the sodium content of this recipe.

Italiana Venison

2 lbs. venison round steak
1/2 cup flour
4 tablespoons vegetable oil
1/8 teaspoon salt
1/8 teaspoon pepper
1 jar spaghetti sauce (26 oz.)
Mozzarella cheese, shredded (8 oz.)
1 onion, sliced
1/2 box of fresh mushrooms, sliced (or 4 oz. can)
Nonstick cooking spray

Slice partially frozen venison tenderloin into 1/4 to 1/2 inch pieces. Pat dry with paper towels. Mix flour with salt and pepper and dip meat in the flour mixture. Brown meat in hot oil. Place half of the meat in a baking dish sprayed with cooking spray. Pour half the spaghetti sauce over the meat and top with half the mozzarella cheese, onion and mushrooms. Repeat with another layer of meat, sauce, cheese, onions and mushrooms. Bake, uncovered, at 350 degrees F for 35 minutes. Yield: 6 servings.

Nutrition Facts

Serving Size 369 g

Amount Per Serving

Calories 648	Calories from Fat 307

	% Daily Value*
Total Fat 34.1g	53%
Saturated Fat 13.0g	65%
Trans Fat 0.0g	
Cholesterol 149mg	50%
Sodium 939mg	39%
Total Carbohydrates 24.3g	8%
Dietary Fiber 3.7g	15%
Sugars 11.4g	
Protein 59.1g	

Vitamin A 13%	Vitamin C 6%
Calcium 31%	Iron 30%

Nutrition Grade B-
* Based on a 2000 calorie diet

Venison Loaf

1/2 cup wild rice
1 lb. ground venison
1/2 lb. ground beef
2 eggs, beaten
1/4 cup onion, chopped
2 tablespoons ketchup
1 teaspoon prepared mustard
1 cup milk
1 teaspoon salt
1/4 teaspoon pepper

Cook the wild rice according to package instructions. Combine the rice with the rest of the ingredients and pack firmly in a greased 8" x 8" pan. Bake at 350 degrees F for one hour. Yield: 4 servings.

Nutrition Facts

Serving Size 291 g

Amount Per Serving

Calories 462	Calories from Fat 149

	% Daily Value*
Total Fat 16.5g	25%
Saturated Fat 7.3g	37%
Trans Fat 0.0g	
Cholesterol 249mg	83%
Sodium 862mg	36%
Total Carbohydrates 20.7g	7%
Dietary Fiber 1.4g	6%
Sugars 5.8g	
Protein 55.2g	

Vitamin A 4%	•	Vitamin C 3%
Calcium 4%	•	Iron 85%

Nutrition Grade B+

* Based on a 2000 calorie diet

Venison Cabbage Rolls

12 large cabbage leaves
1 1/2 lbs. ground venison
4 tablespoons grated onion
1/2 cup butter
2 tablespoons dill, chopped
1 1/2 cups cooked rice
1 tablespoon salt
1/8 teaspoon pepper
3 cups tomato sauce

Brown meat and onion in butter. Mix in the dill, rice, salt and pepper. Place cabbage leaves in boiling water for 1 minute, drain and dry. Spoon about 2 tablespoons of meat mixture in center of leaves and fold the leaf over, tucking in the ends and secure with a toothpick. Place in a 9 x 13" casserole dish and pour tomato sauce over the cabbage rolls. Cover and bake at 325 degrees F for 45 min. Yield: 5 servings.

Nutrition Facts

Serving Size 410 g

Amount Per Serving

Calories 671	Calories from Fat 273
	% Daily Value*
Total Fat 30.3g	**47%**
Saturated Fat 17.2g	**86%**
Cholesterol 182mg	**61%**
Sodium 2415mg	**101%**
Total Carbohydrates 55.8g	**19%**
Dietary Fiber 4.2g	**17%**
Sugars 7.8g	
Protein 42.9g	

Vitamin A 24%	Vitamin C 41%
Calcium 10%	Iron 51%

Nutrition Grade B
* Based on a 2000 calorie diet

Venison Jerky

3 lbs. venison, cut in strips
1/2 cup soy sauce
1/2 cup Worcestershire sauce
1 tablespoon onion salt
1 tablespoon seasoned salt
1 teaspoon black pepper
1 teaspoon garlic salt

Mix all ingredients together, except meat, stirring well to dissolve all salt. Place meat in mix. Marinate in refrigerator overnight, stirring occasionally. Remove from mix, a strip at a time. Place toothpick in one end and hang from oven rack. Turn oven to 150 to 175 degrees F. Prop door open slightly. Bake for 6 to 20 hours. Check frequently so jerky does not become crisp. If too much moisture remains, jerky could mold in humid weather at room temperature. Store in covered glass jars or a plastic bag. Yield: 30 servings.

NUTRITION FACTS PER SERVING (ASSUMING YIELD IS 30 STRIPS OF JERKY):

Nutrition Facts

Serving Size 55 g

Amount Per Serving

Calories 56	Calories from Fat 4
	% Daily Value*
Total Fat 0.5g	1%
Trans Fat 0.0g	
Cholesterol 0mg	0%
Sodium 548mg	23%
Total Carbohydrates 1.2g	0%
Sugars 0.9g	
Protein 10.3g	
Vitamin A 0%	Vitamin C 0%
Calcium 0%	Iron 1%

Nutrition Grade D+
* Based on a 2000 calorie diet

Barbecued Deer Meat

12 venison top round steaks
1 cup celery, chopped
1 cup onions, chopped
1 tablespoon Italian seasoning
1 cup ketchup
1 cup water
1/4 teaspoon salt
1/8 teaspoon pepper

Mix celery, onions, Italian seasoning, ketchup, water, salt and pepper together. Put the steaks in a baking dish or two and pour the mixture over them. Cook at 350 degrees F for 2 hours. With a hand potato masher, mash the meat until it shreds. If needed, cook longer until the meat is tender enough to shred. Serve on hard rolls. Yield: 12 servings.

Nutrition Facts

Serving Size 205 g

Amount Per Serving	
Calories 247	Calories from Fat 29
	% Daily Value*
Total Fat 3.2g	5%
Saturated Fat 1.6g	8%
Cholesterol 123mg	41%
Sodium 347mg	14%
Total Carbohydrates 6.4g	2%
Sugars 5.2g	
Protein 45.9g	

Vitamin A 5%	*	Vitamin C 7%
Calcium 2%	*	Iron 35%

Nutrition Grade A
* Based on a 2000 calorie diet

Wild Game Casserole

1 lb. ground venison, elk or antelope
1 medium onion, diced
1/2 cup wild rice
1 cup brown rice
1 cup condensed cream of chicken or cream of mushroom soup
1 cup water
3 tablespoons soy sauce
2 or 3 stalks of celery, chopped
1 medium carrot, finely chopped
1/2 cup peas

Brown ground venison, elk or antelope. Add onion. Wash and rinse wild rice in hot water and drain; then boil brown rice with the wild rice, until just tender. Meanwhile heat the soup with water together. Add soy sauce and stir well. Then add the celery, carrot, and peas. Mix the soup mixture, rice and meat together, put in a 2 quart greased casserole dish and bake at 350 degrees F for 30 to 45 minutes. Yield: 4 servings.

NUTRITION FACTS PER SERVING (FOR GROUND VENISON):

Nutrition Facts
Serving Size 386 g

Amount Per Serving
Calories 531	Calories from Fat 110

	% Daily Value*
Total Fat 12.2g	19%
Saturated Fat 5.3g	27%
Trans Fat 0.0g	
Cholesterol 114mg	38%
Sodium 1033mg	43%
Total Carbohydrates 64.1g	21%
Dietary Fiber 5.5g	22%
Sugars 4.4g	
Protein 39.8g	

Vitamin A 55%	•	Vitamin C 18%
Calcium 6%	•	Iron 32%

Nutrition Grade A
* Based on a 2000 calorie diet

Deer Chili

4 lbs. ground venison
2 tablespoons vegetable oil
5 cloves minced garlic
2 1/2 tablespoons paprika
5 tablespoons chili powder
1 1/2 tablespoons cumin
1 tablespoon salt
1 tablespoon white pepper
2 quarts water

Brown meat in vegetable oil in a kettle, add garlic, paprika, chili powder, cumin, salt and pepper. Mix in the water. Cover and cook on low heat for 3 hours, stirring occasionally. Add a cup more of water if needed while cooking. Yield: 6 servings.

Nutrition Facts

Serving Size 640 g

Amount Per Serving

Calories 646 — Calories from Fat 281

	% Daily Value*
Total Fat 31.2g	**48%**
Saturated Fat 13.2g	66%
Cholesterol 296mg	**99%**
Sodium 1476mg	**61%**
Total Carbohydrates 7.2g	**2%**
Dietary Fiber 3.7g	15%
Sugars 0.8g	
Protein 81.7g	
Vitamin A 68%	Vitamin C 12%
Calcium 10%	Iron 73%

Nutrition Grade B+
* Based on a 2000 calorie diet

Breaded Venison Steaks

4 venison round steaks
1 cup cracker crumbs
1/2 cup flour
1/8 teaspoon pepper
1 egg
4 tablespoons vegetable oil
1 onion, chopped
1 can mushrooms, drained (4 oz.)
1 cup red wine

Mix the cracker crumbs, flour and pepper together. Beat the egg and coat each steak with egg, then cover with the cracker crumb mixture. Brown the steaks in oil, then place in a baking dish. Cover steaks with onion, mushrooms, and wine. Bake, covered at 350 degrees F for 1 hour and 30 minutes. Yield: 4 servings.

Nutrition Facts

Serving Size 273 g

Amount Per Serving

Calories 492	Calories from Fat 187
	% Daily Value*
Total Fat 20.8g	32%
Saturated Fat 4.0g	20%
Trans Fat 0.1g	
Cholesterol 128mg	43%
Sodium 199mg	8%
Total Carbohydrates 26.6g	9%
Dietary Fiber 1.4g	6%
Sugars 2.5g	
Protein 37.5g	
Vitamin A 1%	Vitamin C 5%
Calcium 4%	Iron 38%

Nutrition Grade C+
* Based on a 2000 calorie diet

Hunter's Stew

1 1/2 lbs. boneless venison
1/2 lb. smoked sausage
2 tablespoons vegetable oil
1/2 cup celery, chopped
1/2 cup onion, chopped
2 cans tomatoes with liquid, chopped (28 oz. each)
1 can beer (12 oz.)
1 teaspoon salt
1 teaspoon sugar
1/2 teaspoon dried rosemary, crushed
1/2 teaspoon dried whole basil
1/2 teaspoon ground pepper
2 carrots, pared and diced
2 medium potatoes, cubed

Cut the venison into 1/2 inch cubes and the sausage into 1/2 inch slices. Brown venison and sausage in hot oil in large Dutch oven. Add onion and celery; cook until tender. Add remaining ingredients, except carrots and potatoes. Reduce heat and simmer for 30 minutes. Add carrots and cook, uncovered for 30 minutes. Add potatoes and cook an additional 30 minutes or until done. Yield: 5 servings.

Nutrition Facts

Serving Size 1415 g

Amount Per Serving

Calories 729	Calories from Fat 203
	% Daily Value*
Total Fat 22.6g	35%
Saturated Fat 6.2g	31%
Trans Fat 0.1g	
Cholesterol 74mg	25%
Sodium 2341mg	98%
Total Carbohydrates 102.3g	34%
Dietary Fiber 24.5g	98%
Sugars 3.7g	
Protein 41.5g	
Vitamin A 240%	Vitamin C 205%
Calcium 42%	Iron 98%

Nutrition Grade A-
* Based on a 2000 calorie diet

Venison Patties

1 lb. ground venison
9 slices bacon, chopped
Small onion, minced
1/2 teaspoon lemon peel, grated
1/8 teaspoon marjoram
1/4 teaspoon salt
1/8 teaspoon pepper
1/8 teaspoon thyme
1 slice bread, crumbled
1 egg

Mix all ingredients together by hand. Form into a 3" roll. Cut into slices. Pour about 2 teaspoons vegetable oil into a skillet to barely cover the bottom. Heat pan until oil is hot.

Fry the patties for 6 to 8 minutes on each side. Yield: 4 servings.

Nutrition Facts
Serving Size 159 g

Amount Per Serving
Calories 318 — Calories from Fat 148

	% Daily Value*
Total Fat 16.4g	25%
Saturated Fat 6.9g	34%
Trans Fat 0.0g	
Cholesterol 168mg	56%
Sodium 596mg	25%
Total Carbohydrates 3.2g	1%
Sugars 0.9g	
Protein 37.0g	

Vitamin A 1%	•	Vitamin C 3%
Calcium 3%	•	Iron 25%

Nutrition Grade B
* Based on a 2000 calorie diet

Hot and Spicy Venison

1 pound venison, back strap

Cut venison, across the grain, into very thin pieces.

Meat Marinade:

3 tablespoons soy sauce
4 teaspoons sherry
2 tablespoons cornstarch
4 teaspoons sesame oil
Dash of white pepper

Soak the venison in the marinade for at least 1/2 hour.

Sauce:

4 tablespoons fresh minced ginger
4 tablespoons fresh minced garlic
4 tablespoons hot bean paste/sauce*
4 tablespoons sweet bean paste*
4 tablespoons soy sauce
4 tablespoons sherry
2 teaspoons rice vinegar
4 teaspoons sugar
2 teaspoons cornstarch

1 large green bell pepper, thinly sliced
1 large onion, cut into small cubes
4 whole dried red chili peppers
3 tablespoons peanut oil, divided

Combine sauce ingredients in a bowl, mixing well. Heat wok, adding 1 tablespoon of peanut oil. Stir fry green pepper with onion for 2 minutes. Add a pinch of salt and 1/4 teaspoons of pepper to taste, set aside. Add 1-2 tablespoons of peanut oil, and add whole dried red chili peppers. Let cook for 20 seconds, and add venison. Stir fry venison for 1 minute. Add sauce, and stir until thick. Add the vegetables back into the wok just long enough to reheat. Serve over rice. (Venison should be cut like a flank steak. When thinly sliced across the grain and cooked quickly, it becomes juicy and tender.) Yield: 4 servings.

These products can be purchased in an Oriental market.

Nutrition Facts

Serving Size 291 g

Amount Per Serving

Calories 421 — Calories from Fat 163

	% Daily Value*
Total Fat 18.1g	**28%**
Saturated Fat 2.5g	**12%**
Trans Fat 0.0g	
Cholesterol 0mg	**0%**
Sodium 3031mg	**126%**
Total Carbohydrates 30.9g	**10%**
Dietary Fiber 3.8g	**15%**
Sugars 13.4g	
Protein 32.1g	

Vitamin A 29% • Vitamin C 97%
Calcium 5% • Iron 14%

Nutrition Grade B

* Based on a 2000 calorie diet

Wisconsin Venison Sausage

1 cup water
1 lb. ground venison
1 lb. ground beef
2 1/2 teaspoons liquid smoke
2 1/2 teaspoons garlic powder
1 teaspoon onion powder
1 1/2 teaspoons Morton Tender Quick® salt (do not substitute)
Dash of black pepper

Mix all ingredients together. Divide in 3 equal parts and roll in aluminum foil (1 1/2 inch diameter). Refrigerate 24 hours before baking. Remove foil, bake at 325 degrees F for 1 1/2 hours. Pat dry with paper towels. Rewrap in foil and refrigerate or freeze. Serve in thin slices.

Nutrition Facts

Serving Size 388 g

Amount Per Serving	
Calories 574	Calories from Fat 197
	% Daily Value*
Total Fat 21.9g	34%
Saturated Fat 9.6g	48%
Cholesterol 283mg	94%
Sodium 221mg	9%
Total Carbohydrates 2.3g	1%
Sugars 0.8g	
Protein 86.3g	
Vitamin A 0%	Vitamin C 1%
Calcium 3%	Iron 187%

Nutrition Grade B
* Based on a 2000 calorie diet

No Wild Taste Meat Loaf

2 lbs. ground venison
1 bottle seafood cocktail sauce (12 oz.)
1/3 cup water
1 large egg
1 medium onion, chopped
1 1/2 cups crackers or cornflakes, crushed

Mix all together and put in a greased loaf pan. Bake covered at 350 degrees F for 1 hour and 10 minutes. Uncover for the last 10 to 15 minutes. Yield: 6 servings.

NUTRITION FACTS PER SERVING: (USING CRACKERS):

Nutrition Facts

Serving Size 263 g

Amount Per Serving

Calories 455	Calories from Fat 155

	% Daily Value*
Total Fat 17.2g	26%
Saturated Fat 6.9g	35%
Trans Fat 0.1g	
Cholesterol 179mg	60%
Sodium 945mg	39%
Total Carbohydrates 29.2g	10%
Dietary Fiber 0.6g	2%
Sugars 17.6g	
Protein 43.1g	

Vitamin A 1%	•	Vitamin C 2%
Calcium 5%	•	Iron 32%

Nutrition Grade B
* Based on a 2000 calorie diet

Venison Steak Fromage

2 venison steaks or backstrap
1/3 cup flour
1/4 teaspoon garlic salt
1/2 teaspoon salt
1/8 teaspoon pepper
3 tablespoons vegetable oil
3/4 cup water
1/3 cup onion, chopped
1/3 cup Cheddar cheese, grated
2 tablespoons parsley

Pound the venison with a meat tenderizer to soften the meat. Cut venison into 1" pieces. Combine flour, garlic salt, salt and pepper. Dredge steak in flour mixture, then brown the meat in hot vegetable oil. Add water and onions; sprinkle remaining flour mixture over the top. Cover; simmer for 1/2 hour. Remove cover. Sprinkle on grated cheese and parsley. Yield: 2 servings.

Nutrition Facts

Serving Size 276 g

Amount Per Serving

Calories 498 — Calories from Fat 260

	% Daily Value*
Total Fat 28.9g	44%
Saturated Fat 9.1g	45%
Cholesterol 106mg	35%
Sodium 750mg	31%
Total Carbohydrates 18.5g	6%
Dietary Fiber 1.1g	4%
Sugars 1.1g	
Protein 39.3g	

Vitamin A 10% • Vitamin C 11%
Calcium 16% • Iron 32%

Nutrition Grade B
* Based on a 2000 calorie diet

Slow Cooker Venison

1 1/2 lbs. venison
1/3 cup chicken broth
Can of sliced mushrooms (4 oz.)
1/2 pkg. onion soup mix
1 can cream of mushroom soup (10.5 oz.)
1/2 cup sour cream

Cut the venison into 1 inch pieces and put in slow cooker. Mix together the chicken broth, mushrooms, onion soup and cream of mushroom soup and pour over venison. Cook for 9 to 11 hours on low; turn slow cooker to high and cook for one more hour. Add 1/2 cup of sour cream before serving. Serve over noodles. Yield: 4 servings.

Nutrition Facts

Serving Size 322 g

Amount Per Serving

Calories 286	Calories from Fat 91
	% Daily Value*
Total Fat 10.1g	**15%**
Saturated Fat 4.3g	**21%**
Cholesterol 13mg	**4%**
Sodium 317mg	**13%**
Total Carbohydrates 4.7g	**2%**
Sugars 1.1g	
Protein 40.2g	

Vitamin A 4%	•	Vitamin C 2%
Calcium 4%	•	Iron 7%

Nutrition Grade C
* Based on a 2000 calorie diet

ELK RECIPES

Elk

Tips for Cooking Elk

Not many hunters get an opportunity to hunt elk. However, if you're one of the fortunate few and are a successful shot, you'll come home with some great meat that you can use for steaks, roasts, kabobs, stews and ground meat recipes.

Elk meat is very lean and nutritious. It has only 2.1 grams of fat in roughly four ounces of meat. It is one of the leanest meats available, and those four ounces of meat have only 165 calories. Compare that to beef, which averages 230 calories or pork's average 212 calories. Even venison has about 3 grams of fat and has comparable calories. Elk is a great protein source for health conscious consumers who must watch their fat intake.

Aging Elk

Aging tenderizes meat by allowing natural enzymes produced by bacteria to break down the long proteins of the meat. This action produces shorter proteins that are more tender and easy to eat.

Keep the meat near freezing for three to five days to tenderize it. However, the longer the meat is above freezing, the more moisture it will lose.

Leave the frozen meat in the refrigerator to thaw completely, and then leave it there for 24 hours for an easy way to complete the aging process.

Marinating Elk

Marinating is a great way to add flavor to your meat, as well as tenderizing the flesh for a succulent and moist meal. For best results with any marinade, the meat should be totally submerged in the liquid, and it should remain overnight in the refrigerator.

Always marinate your meat in the refrigerator. Allowing the meat to sit at room temperature does not speed up the marinating process and increases the risk of bacterial growth.

Buttermilk is a standard marinade for wild game, and elk is no exception.

Italian dressing, with its oil and vinegar is a great, easy marinade that doesn't require any preparation and adds lots of flavor with no extra work.

An excellent way to ensure that your roast is thoroughly marinated is to butterfly it open to a thickness of one inch. Marinate for the prescribed amount of time. When the roast is ready to cook, stuff the meat with herbs, garlic and spices. Now, roll it back up and tie with several pieces of kitchen twine to secure it. Cook and prepare to enjoy a perfectly flavored roast.

Your favorite adult beverage can be used in a marinade for just about any meat. Beer, wine, liquors and liqueurs are all great ingredients for marinades.

Reducing the Gamey Taste of Elk

Aging and marinating will minimize much of the gamey taste associated with wild meat. Patience is a virtue when marinating and aging meat. You must give the meat the suggested time for the process to do its work. Don't shortchange the aging or marinating time and you'll wind up with a tender and flavorful entrée that everyone will enjoy.

Beyond marinating and aging, there are a couple other things you can do to reduce that distinct flavor associated with wild meat.

We know that elk doesn't have much fat content. However, there will be areas of meat that have a thin layer of fat. This fat is one of the culprits that gives wild meat a gamey taste. Cut away as much of the visible fat as possible from the flesh and you'll reduce that unappetizing gamey taste.

The other offender is the silvery membrane you will find surrounding areas of flesh. Use a sharp knife to slide under the membrane and use your fingers to peel it away from the meat.

General Tips for Cooking Elk

To add moisture to an elk roast, make deep slits in the flesh and add pork grease, butter or oil. The deep slits allow the oil to seep through the meat. You can also deep season meat this way. Insert slivers of fresh garlic to add flavor to your roast.

Salt pork, either diced or sliced in thin strips, adds moisture and flavor to elk meat.

An unusual roasting liquid for elk, or any red meat, is a can of cola. Use the regular sugar version, and save the sugar-free can for yourself. Simply pour a can of cola in your roaster, add your elk meat and cook as usual.

Fast cooking is best for dry cooking methods. Quickly sear the meat on both sides to seal in the juices, and cook to no more than medium for best texture and moisture content.

Use tongs to turn grilled or fried meat. Piercing meat with a fork allows the juices to escape and the meat will dry out.

Sear meat quickly in a hot, oiled pan to seal in the juices before roasting.

Meat injectors are a quick and easy way to add flavor and moisture to your meat.

Cooking Times for Elk

There are two methods of roasting elk. The fast method ensures that the meat will not dry out from prolonged cooking. This is great for young meat that is naturally tender. The slow method allows the meat to become tender from long cooking at a low temperature. This method is suitable for tougher cuts of meat.

Fast Method

Brown the roast on all sides. Place the meat in a shallow roaster and baste with oil. Cook in a 450 degree Fahrenheit oven for 10 to 14 minutes per pound. Allow the meat to rest 20 minutes before serving.

Slow Method

Use a sharp knife to make several deep slits in the roast. Insert slivers of pork or beef fat into the holes. You can also use butter, margarine or oil. Quickly brown the meat all over to seal in the juices, place in a covered roasting pan, add cooking liquid and roast at 200 degrees Fahrenheit for 45 minutes per pound. Add an extra 45 minutes to your cooking time. Baste frequently and use the basting juices to make gravy.

Elk Steak Internal Temperature

Rare: 104 degrees Fahrenheit

Medium Rare: 111 degrees Fahrenheit

Medium: 129 degrees Fahrenheit

Use a medium heat and a heavy skillet to fry elk steak. Use olive oil to brown the meat. Use medium heat to grill and remove the steak 5 degrees before it reaches the desired temperature. Allow the meat to rest. The meat will continue cooking to its final desired temperature.

Elk Roast Internal Temperature

Rare: 135 degrees Fahrenheit

Medium Rare: 136 degrees Fahrenheit

Medium: 140 degrees Fahrenheit

For best results, take the roast out of the oven when the temperature is 5 degrees lower than your desired temperature. Quickly wrap the meat in aluminum foil and let it rest for 10 to 15 minutes. This allows the juices to set while the meat continues to cook to the proper temperature.

Roasted Elk with Lingonberry Sauce

1 large elk or venison roast, about 4 pounds
2 medium onions, quartered
6 carrots, peeled and cut into pieces
6 stalks celery, cut into pieces
2 bay leaves, whole
1/8 teaspoon salt
1/8 teaspoon pepper
Lingonberry Sauce (recipe below)

Preheat the oven to 300 degrees F. Place the roast in a deep, heavy baking pan. Add all the vegetables and seasonings to the roasting pan and pour in enough water to completely cover the roast. Cover and bake in the oven for 5 to 6 hours. When the meat is done, discard the broth, remove the vegetables and place the meat on a heated platter. Serve *Lingonberry Sauce* over the roast. Yield: 6 servings.

Lingonberry Sauce:

1 jar Lingonberries in syrup, (7 oz.)
3 ounces currant jelly
1 tablespoon Worcestershire sauce
2 tablespoons lemon juice
3 dashes hot pepper sauce
1/8 teaspoon salt
1/8 teaspoon pepper

Combine all the ingredients in a small saucepan and mix well. Bring to a boil and reduce the heat. Simmer for 3 to 5 minutes to blend flavors. Good served over antelope, venison, or duck. *Note: Lingonberries are the Scandinavian cranberry.*

Nutrition Facts

Serving Size 506 g

Amount Per Serving

Calories 505　　　　　Calories from Fat 55

　　　　　　　　　　　　　　　　　% Daily Value*

Total Fat 6.1g	**9%**
Saturated Fat 2.2g	**11%**
Trans Fat 0.0g	
Cholesterol 221mg	**74%**
Sodium 321mg	**13%**
Total Carbohydrates 14.8g	**5%**
Dietary Fiber 3.3g	**13%**
Sugars 8.4g	
Protein 92.7g	

Vitamin A 206%　　•　　Vitamin C 25%
Calcium 6%　　　　•　　Iron 64%

Nutrition Grade B

* Based on a 2000 calorie diet

Silver Bow Elk

2 1/2 pounds elk, trimmed
1 cup all-purpose flour
1/8 cup vegetable oil
1 cup mushrooms, sliced
1 shallot, finely chopped
1/4 cup brandy
1/2 cup red wine
2 cups beef stock
1 teaspoon freshly ground black pepper

Garnish:
2 ounces hazelnuts ground
2 strips bacon, crisply cooked and crumbled

Cut the elk into 18 medallions and pound with a mallet to tenderize. Dredge the medallions in flour. Heat oil in a skillet and brown both sides of the medallions, a few at a time, and set aside. To the skillet, add the mushrooms, shallot, and brandy and sauté for 1 minute. Add the red wine. Cook over high heat until the alcohol has evaporated. Add the beef stock and pepper. Reduce the liquid over high heat for 3 to 4 minutes.

Add the elk to the skillet and cook to desired doneness. Remove to a heated platter. Reduce the sauce by cooking over high heat until syrupy. Pour the sauce over the elk, garnish with ground hazelnuts and bacon, and serve. Yield: Serves 6.

Nutrition Facts

Serving Size 344 g

Amount Per Serving

Calories 512　　　　Calories from Fat 152

　　　　　　　　　　　　　　　　% Daily Value*

Total Fat 16.9g	**26%**
Saturated Fat 3.6g	**18%**
Trans Fat 0.0g	
Cholesterol 145mg	**48%**
Sodium 525mg	**22%**
Total Carbohydrates 19.0g	**6%**
Dietary Fiber 1.7g	**7%**
Sugars 0.8g	
Protein 64.3g	

Vitamin A 1%	Vitamin C 2%
Calcium 3%	Iron 50%

Nutrition Grade C

* Based on a 2000 calorie diet

Slow Cooker Elk Enchiladas

1 lb. ground elk
1 cup onion, chopped
1/2 cup green pepper, chopped
1 can pinto or kidney beans, drained and rinsed (16 oz.)
1 can black beans, drained and rinsed (15 oz.)
1 can diced tomatoes with green chilies, undrained (10 oz.)
1/3 cup water
1/2 teaspoon cumin
3/4 teaspoon chili powder
1/2 teaspoon salt
1/4 teaspoon pepper
1 1/2 cups Cheddar cheese, shredded
1 1/2 cups Monterey Jack cheese, shredded
6 corn tortillas

In a frying pan, cook meat, green pepper and onion until meat is cooked. Drain the fat. Add the beans, tomatoes, water, cumin, chili powder, pepper and salt and bring to a boil. Reduce heat; cover and simmer for 15 minutes. Mix the cheeses together in a bowl. In a slow cooker, put 1/2 cup of the meat mixture, one tortilla, then 1/2 cup cheese. Repeat the layers. Cover and cook on low for 5 to 7 hours. Yield: 4 servings.

NUTRITION FACTS PER SERVING: (BASED ON 2/3 CUP OF ELK PER SERVING)

Nutrition Facts

Serving Size 586 g

Amount Per Serving

Calories 851	Calories from Fat 346
	% Daily Value*
Total Fat 38.4g	59%
Saturated Fat 21.7g	109%
Trans Fat 0.0g	
Cholesterol 171mg	57%
Sodium 1613mg	67%
Total Carbohydrates 63.1g	21%
Dietary Fiber 16.7g	67%
Sugars 6.6g	
Protein 67.2g	
Vitamin A 28%	Vitamin C 32%
Calcium 78%	Iron 53%

Nutrition Grade B-

* Based on a 2000 calorie diet

Game Meat Italian Sausage

10 lbs. elk and/or deer trimmings
10 lbs. pork butt
2 tablespoons coarsely ground black pepper
1 ounce fennel seeds
Salt, garlic powder, and hot pepper flakes to taste

Coarsely grind both meats. Mix together by hand. Spread on flat surface. Pat to 1-inch thickness. Salt surface heavily. Sprinkle fennel seeds over all. Sprinkle black pepper, garlic, and pepper flakes over all. With hands, fold into mix. Mix heartily. Have a beer. Make a patty, fry it, and taste. Adjust the seasonings. Test again. Make into patties or put in casings, twisting every 5 inches. Freeze.

NUTRITION FACTS PER SERVING: (BASED ON 1 LB. PER SERVING)
776 CALORIES
19.7G TOTAL FAT
139.3G PROTEIN

The nutrition chart is not available for this recipe since the amount of salt used cannot be estimated correctly.

Hearty Elk Chili

2 lbs. ground elk meat
1/2 cup onion, diced
3 cloves of garlic, minced
2 cans diced tomatoes (14 1/2 oz. each)
1 can pork and beans (28 oz.)
3 tablespoons chunky salsa
1 1/4 tablespoons brown sugar
3 teaspoons chili powder
1/2 teaspoon black pepper
1/2 teaspoon garlic salt

Cook elk meat and diced onion in a Dutch oven until meat is well done and no longer pink in color. Add garlic salt and cook 1 more minute, drain. Mix in the rest of the ingredients (do not drain tomatoes or pork & beans) and bring to a boil. Reduce heat and let simmer for at least 2 hours. Yield: 6 servings.

Nutrition Facts

Serving Size 443 g

Amount Per Serving

Calories 478 — Calories from Fat 140

	% Daily Value*
Total Fat 15.5g	24%
Saturated Fat 6.9g	34%
Cholesterol 127mg	42%
Sodium 959mg	40%
Total Carbohydrates 36.1g	12%
Dietary Fiber 9.1g	36%
Sugars 5.6g	
Protein 48.7g	

Vitamin A 23%	•	Vitamin C 23%
Calcium 12%	•	Iron 46%

Nutrition Grade A-
* Based on a 2000 calorie diet

BBQ Elk Meatballs

1 lb. ground elk
1/2 cup whole milk
1/2 teaspoon table salt
3/4 cup rolled oats, uncooked
1/2 cup onion, minced

Combine all of the above ingredients in a bowl.

Sauce:
1 cup ketchup
1/2 cup water
1/2 cup onion, diced
2 tablespoons vinegar
1/4 cup brown sugar

Roll 1 inch balls out of meat mixture and place on a shallow cooking sheet (9 x 13 inches). In a mixing bowl, combine all of the ingredients for the sauce and pour over meatballs. Bake uncovered at 350 degrees F for 1 hour, turning over twice. Yield: 4 servings.

Nutrition Facts

Serving Size 295 g

Amount Per Serving

Calories 401 — Calories from Fat 109

	% Daily Value*
Total Fat 12.1g	**19%**
Saturated Fat 5.3g	**27%**
Trans Fat 0.0g	
Cholesterol 92mg	**31%**
Sodium 1074mg	**45%**
Total Carbohydrates 38.5g	**13%**
Dietary Fiber 2.2g	**9%**
Sugars 25.4g	
Protein 34.6g	

Vitamin A 12%	Vitamin C 19%
Calcium 8%	Iron 27%

Nutrition Grade B+
* Based on a 2000 calorie diet

Country Elk Meatloaf

1 1/2 lbs. ground elk
2 large eggs
1 can tomato sauce (8 oz.)
1 onion, chopped
1 1/4 cups dried bread crumbs
1 teaspoon salt
1/8 teaspoon black pepper
1/4 cup brown sugar
3 tablespoons spicy brown mustard
3 tablespoons apple cider vinegar

Place the 2 eggs in a large bowl and beat until well mixed. Add onion, tomato sauce, salt, pepper and bread crumbs; mix well. Add the ground elk and mix again. Press mixture into an ungreased loaf pan measuring 9 x 5 x 3 inches. Mix together the mustard, brown sugar and vinegar and pour over the formed meatloaf. Leave uncovered and bake at 350 degrees F for 1 hour and 10 minutes. Yield: 4 servings.

Nutrition Facts

Serving Size 342 g

Amount Per Serving

Calories 559	Calories from Fat 174

% Daily Value*

Total Fat 19.3g	30%
Saturated Fat 8.0g	40%
Trans Fat 0.0g	
Cholesterol 226mg	75%
Sodium 1399mg	58%
Total Carbohydrates 39.1g	13%
Dietary Fiber 2.9g	11%
Sugars 14.7g	
Protein 54.0g	

Vitamin A 6%	Vitamin C 10%
Calcium 11%	Iron 47%

Nutrition Grade B+

* Based on a 2000 calorie diet

DOVE RECIPES

Dove and Quail

Tips for Cooking Dove

Whether you call them Mourning Doves, Turtle Doves or Rain Doves, these birds are some of the most widespread and abundant in the United States. It is also the leading game bird for both sport and meat. Fortunately, these prolific little birds may lay as many as six broods in a single year, so you're likely to come home with a nice bunch.

Dove is wonderful for preparing entrees, appetizers and special snacks. These tasty game birds have 13 grams of fat and 216 calories for a 3.5 ounce portion of meat.

Marinating Dove

Since dove can have a gamey taste, it's a good idea to marinate the meat. Brining overnight helps to disperse the gamey taste and tenderize the meat. If you don't brine the meat long enough, the salt doesn't have time to completely penetrate the flesh. Overnight or 10 to 12 hours is required for proper brining. One tablespoon of salt per quart of cold water is a basic solution.

A tried and true old standby is bottled Italian dressing. Not only do the ingredients tame the gamey flavor, but the spices add a lot of tang to the meat.

Buttermilk is a universal marinade for gamey meat and many cooks use it for dove.

Teriyaki is often used to mask and minimize the strong taste of wild meat and it is often used with dove meat.

Cooking Tips For Dove

You'll need at least two to three doves per person when planning your menu and guest list.

Stuff the body cavity of a dove with peeled grapes, jalapeno pepper or any flavorful fruit or savory vegetable to add extra taste to a roasted bird. Baste with butter and cook at 350 degrees Fahrenheit until done.

Another savory ingredient combo to add to a dove body cavity is a slice of pancetta and a sage leaf.

Barding the breast of a dove adds oil and retains moisture in the meat. Bard the breast with either fatback or bacon. Remove the barding shortly before the meat is done to allow time for browning. Bacon and salt pork add flavor to the meat, while plain fat merely adds oil and preserves moisture.

To hold thin sheets of fatback in place, wrap the fat around the meat and secure with kitchen twine.

Wrap doves in buttered grape leaves, and attach thin slices of salt pork. Skewer the birds and roast over coals 10 to 15 minutes.

Dove meat does not age well, so cook and serve it as soon as possible.

Roasting and Grilling

Always use a medium heat when grilling dove. Don't overcook the meat, as overdone dove may have a liver-like taste and texture. The meat should still have a touch of pinkness to it.

Use a fish-grilling basket to easily cook all the meat at one time. It's simple to turn the meat over and monitor it for doneness.

Roasting should be done quickly at 375 degrees Fahrenheit and the meat should not be allowed to overcook. Basting or wrapping in bacon or lard will help keep the meat moist.

Quail Chasseur

8 quail
1/4 teaspoon salt
1/8 teaspoon pepper
1/2 cup flour
1/2 cup margarine
3 cups chicken stock
1/4 teaspoon dried thyme
1 bay leaf
3/4 cup dry white wine

Rinse and dry quail. Mix the flour, salt and pepper. Sprinkle inside and out with flour mixture. Melt margarine in large skillet, add quail. Brown the quail on all sides over medium heat. Add stock, thyme, bay leaf and wine. Cover tightly and simmer over low heat for 30 minutes or until birds are tender. Serve with pan juices poured over quail. Yield: 4 servings.

Nutrition Facts

Serving Size 472 g

Amount Per Serving

Calories 744 — Calories from Fat 461

	% Daily Value*
Total Fat 51.3g	79%
Saturated Fat 11.8g	59%
Cholesterol 170mg	57%
Sodium 1109mg	46%
Total Carbohydrates 14.0g	5%
Sugars 0.9g	
Protein 48.4g	

Vitamin A 32%	Vitamin C 20%
Calcium 7%	Iron 56%

Nutrition Grade F
* Based on a 2000 calorie diet

Dove or Quail Casserole

6 doves or quail
1/2 cup butter
1 can cream of mushroom soup (10.5 oz.)
Sour cream (8 oz.)

Brown birds in butter; reserve drippings. Place birds in greased 1 quart casserole dish. Mix mushroom soup and sour cream with drippings and pour over browned birds. Bake, covered, at 350 degrees F for 1 hour and 15 minutes. Yield: 3 servings.

Nutrition Facts

Serving Size 288 g

Amount Per Serving

Calories 635	Calories from Fat 492

	% Daily Value*
Total Fat 54.7g	**84%**
Saturated Fat 30.0g	**150%**
Cholesterol 115mg	**38%**
Sodium 573mg	**24%**
Total Carbohydrates 6.5g	**2%**
Sugars 0.8g	
Protein 30.7g	

Vitamin A 29%	•	Vitamin C 1%
Calcium 10%	•	Iron 3%

Nutrition Grade D
* Based on a 2000 calorie diet

Spicy Dove Poppers

6 dove breasts, deboned
1 can jalapeno peppers, whole (7 oz.)
Cream cheese (8 oz.)
6 pieces of bacon

Preheat the grill. Run water over dove breasts and pat dry. Cut jalapenos in half lengthwise and remove veins and all of the seeds. Press a portion of the cream cheese into the jalapeno half and add the dove breast on top. Top with the other half of the jalapeno, wrap with bacon and secure with a wooden toothpick. Repeat until all poppers are secured and ready for grilling. Grill 15 to 20 minutes until bacon is crispy and dove is cooked through, turning poppers once. (Can also be baked in 350 degree F oven. Bake 15 to 20 minutes, turn doves, and bake 10 minutes more, or until bacon is crisp.) Yield: 3 servings.

NUTRITION FACTS PER SERVING: (BASED ON 8 OZ. DOVE BREASTS, SERVING SIZE OF 2 BREASTS PER PERSON)

Nutrition Facts

Serving Size 453 g

Amount Per Serving

Calories 493	Calories from Fat 330
	% Daily Value*
Total Fat 36.7g	56%
Saturated Fat 20.6g	103%
Cholesterol 163mg	54%
Sodium 1512mg	63%
Total Carbohydrates 2.0g	1%
Protein 35.0g	

Vitamin A 21%	•	Vitamin C 19%
Calcium 7%	•	Iron 19%

Nutrition Grade C+

* Based on a 2000 calorie diet

Note: Use low sodium bacon to lower the sodium content of this recipe.

Quail in Orange Sauce

8 quail, cleaned and skinned
1/8 cup margarine, melted
1 cup orange marmalade
1/4 cup brown sugar
3 tablespoons wine vinegar
2 teaspoons Worcestershire sauce
1 teaspoon salt
1/2 teaspoon ground ginger
1/2 teaspoon curry powder
1/8 teaspoon salt
1/8 teaspoon pepper
1/8 teaspoon cayenne pepper

Wash and dry quail and place in a 13 x 9" baking pan. Brush with melted margarine. Mix the remaining ingredients in a saucepan; cook over medium-high heat until sauce boils. Cook for 2 minutes, stirring constantly. Remove from heat; baste quail with sauce. Cook at 350 degrees F for 20 minutes, basting occasionally with sauce. Flip the quail; cook for an additional 20 minutes. Yield: 4 servings.

NUTRITION FACTS PER SERVING: (BASED ON 2- 8 OZ. QUAIL PER PERSON)

Nutrition Facts

Serving Size 372 g

Amount Per Serving

Calories 706	Calories from Fat 175
	% Daily Value*
Total Fat 19.5g	30%
Saturated Fat 0.9g	5%
Trans Fat 0.0g	
Cholesterol 0mg	0%
Sodium 947mg	39%
Total Carbohydrates 77.1g	26%
Dietary Fiber 1.5g	6%
Sugars 58.1g	
Protein 70.9g	

Vitamin A 7%	•	Vitamin C 10%
Calcium 4%	•	Iron 2%

Nutrition Grade C-
* Based on a 2000 calorie diet

Grilled BBQ Dove

10 dove breasts, whole
1/2 cup onion, diced
1 teaspoon garlic, minced
1/4 cup butter
1/4 cup barbeque sauce
1/3 cup beer, light or regular

In a large bowl, mix together all of the above ingredients except for the dove breasts. Place all 10 breasts on a large piece of aluminum foil, top with barbeque mixture and wrap tightly. Turn foil packet over several times while grilling 20 to 30 minutes over medium heat. Yield: 5 servings.

NUTRITION FACTS PER SERVING: (USING LIGHT BEER, 8 OZ. DOVE BREASTS, SERVING SIZE OF 2 BREASTS PER PERSON)

Nutrition Facts

Serving Size 148 g

Amount Per Serving

Calories 243	Calories from Fat 113

	% Daily Value*
Total Fat 12.6g	19%
Saturated Fat 6.8g	34%
Trans Fat 0.0g	
Cholesterol 89mg	30%
Sodium 267mg	11%
Total Carbohydrates 5.8g	2%
Sugars 3.8g	
Protein 25.6g	

Vitamin A 7%	•	Vitamin C 11%
Calcium 2%	•	Iron 15%

Nutrition Grade B
* Based on a 2000 calorie diet

Smothered Doves

3 dove breasts
1/4 teaspoon salt
1/8 teaspoon pepper
1/2 cup flour
1/2 cup vegetable oil
4 teaspoons Worcestershire sauce
4 teaspoons lemon juice
1 cup water

Salt and pepper the doves. Put flour in a paper bag. Drop the dove breasts into flour. Close bag; shake well. Pour oil in skillet. Fry doves in oil until golden brown. Put 1/2 teaspoon lemon juice on top of each dove. Add 1 cup water; cover skillet. Simmer for 1 hour or until tender. Add water if necessary. Yield: 2 servings.

NUTRITION FACTS PER SERVING: (BASED ON 8 OZ. DOVE BREASTS, SERVING SIZE OF 1 1/2 BREASTS PER PERSON)

Nutrition Facts

Serving Size 406 g

Amount Per Serving

Calories 665	Calories from Fat 217
	% Daily Value*
Total Fat 24.2g	37%
Saturated Fat 5.8g	29%
Trans Fat 0.0g	
Cholesterol 197mg	66%
Sodium 591mg	25%
Total Carbohydrates 26.1g	9%
Dietary Fiber 0.9g	4%
Sugars 2.3g	
Protein 80.2g	
Vitamin A 3%	Vitamin C 37%
Calcium 4%	Iron 52%

Nutrition Grade B+
* Based on a 2000 calorie diet

Marinated Doves

30 doves
1 package shrimp boil (5 oz.)

Boil doves in shrimp boil for 45 minutes to remove wild flavor; drain. Place doves in a 13 x 9" baking pan. Mix ingredients below for the dove barbecue sauce together in a sauce pan, and boil for 3 to 5 minutes:

Dove Barbecue Sauce

1 pint white wine vinegar
5 oz. Worcestershire sauce
1 cup vegetable oil
1/2 cup sugar
1/8 teaspoon salt
1/8 teaspoon pepper
Dash of Tabasco sauce

Pour half the barbeque sauce over doves and marinate in refrigerator for 4 hours or overnight. Bake birds in the remaining sauce at 350 degrees F for 30 minutes, or until lightly browned. Yield: 15 servings.

NUTRITION FACTS PER SERVING: (BASED ON 2- 8 OZ. BREASTS PER PERSON, INCLUDING ALL THE BBQ SAUCE THE DOVE WAS COOKED IN)

Nutrition Facts

Serving Size 484 g

Amount Per Serving

Calories 1,046	Calories from Fat 351
	% Daily Value*
Total Fat 39.0g	60%
Saturated Fat 1.4g	7%
Trans Fat 0.0g	
Cholesterol 0mg	0%
Sodium 62mg	3%
Total Carbohydrates 4.2g	1%
Sugars 4.2g	
Protein 163.3g	
Vitamin A 0%	Vitamin C 0%
Calcium 0%	Iron 0%

Nutrition Grade D+

* Based on a 2000 calorie diet

Baked Dove

6 dove breasts
1/4 teaspoon salt
1/8 teaspoon pepper
6 tablespoons butter
3 tablespoons flour
2 cups chicken broth
1/2 cup cooking sherry
1 cup canned mushrooms, sliced
1/4 cup parsley, minced

Debone dove breasts and cut into halves. Season with salt and pepper. In a skillet, melt butter and brown dove breasts. Remove breasts from skillet and place in a baking dish. Mix the 3 tablespoons of flour with the butter in skillet, stir well and let brown. Slowly pour in cooking sherry and chicken broth. Pour over breast in baking dish, add parsley and mushrooms. Cover and bake at 350 degrees F for 1 hour. Yield: 3 servings.

NUTRITION FACTS PER SERVING: (BASED ON 2-8 OZ. BREASTS PER PERSON)

Nutrition Facts

Serving Size 718 g

Amount Per Serving

Calories 855	Calories from Fat 339
	% Daily Value*
Total Fat 37.7g	**58%**
Saturated Fat 18.8g	**94%**
Cholesterol 324mg	**108%**
Sodium 1122mg	**47%**
Total Carbohydrates 8.8g	**3%**
Dietary Fiber 0.6g	**3%**
Sugars 1.2g	
Protein 107.7g	

Vitamin A 26%	•	Vitamin C 51%
Calcium 7%	•	Iron 69%

Nutrition Grade C+

* Based on a 2000 calorie diet

DUCK RECIPES

Duck

Tips for Cooking Duck

Duck from the store and wild duck are two quite different animals when it comes to cooking. Yes, both have webbed feet and have a cute little waddle when they walk, but a domestic duck has spent a life of leisure eating and growing fat, while a wild duck spends most of his time foraging and migrating.

Duck meat is not terribly high in calories. A three ounce portion of skinless breast meat contains only three grams of fat and has 119 calories. It's all that fat that packs on the calories, and wild ducks don't have nearly as much as their portly, domesticated cousins.

Wild duck has a stronger flavor than domestic duck, and they have dark, rich meat. The fat content of a wild duck is related to the time of the year. After returning from their migration, ducks have very little fat. As they spend time grazing and regaining their weight, the fat content of the duck increases. Wild duck are not nearly as meaty as domestic duck, and at most, one duck will feed two people.

Your method of duck preparation should be based on the type of duck you've brought home. Where they live and what they eat play a big role in how they taste. Shallow water duck like mallard and teal eat a grain based diet. They have a rich, mellow flavor and are well suited for roasting. Ducks who live near the ocean are fish eaters. These breeds can have fishy tasting flesh. Ducks such as eider, scoters, mergansers and goldeneyes are all fish eating birds, and they should be prepared to minimize or conceal the fishy taste.

Removing the Fishy or Gamey Taste from Duck

If you've come home with ducks that are elderly or have definite fish-breath, it's a good idea to marinate them. This removes some of the gamey or fishy taste, and the process tenderizes aging duck meat. Packing the cavities with onion and lemon and aging the carcasses for a couple days is also a long-used method for removing strong tastes from a duck. After removing and discarding the lemon and onion, wash out the cavity with cold water before cooking.

The fat of a duck holds a lot of flavor, so if you're concerned with a strong taste, remove as much of the fat as you can. This will cut down on the sharp flavor considerably. Fat content in domestic duck is much higher than its wild counterpart, but since the fat of a domestic bird doesn't have an intense flavor, it is usually left in place. To remove the fat of a domestic bird, the skin is usually scored so the fat can drip out as it liquefies in the cooking process.

Marinate Your Duck

Wine, vinegar and buttermilk are all contenders for this job, and there are tons of marinade recipes available. Soaking the meat overnight in tomato juice is a popular method to tenderize the flesh and flavor the meat, as its acidity breaks down the tissue.

Thyme, rosemary and other herbs used with poultry are great additions to your duck marinade. Both sweet and citrus fruits add additional layers of flavor, along with old standbys like onion, celery, carrot and garlic.

Feel free to customize a marinade recipe, and remove or add other spices and herbs. However, don't shortchange yourself in the time department. The liquids need time to break down the tissue, which tenderizes the meat. Also, the seasonings require time to permeate the flesh.

It's not a good idea to add salt to your marinade, as it draws moisture and your wild duck may be dry fleshed. On the other hand, if your bird has shot damage, salt will help to draw clotted blood from the meat.

General Cooking Tips

Duck should be served medium rare or rare to preserve its flavor and tenderness. Overcooked duck will be tough and stringy. You can bet no one will be asking for seconds of overcooked duck.

If you're roasting duck, place a few strips of bacon across the bird. It adds to the flavor, but more importantly, it adds oil to make the meat moister.

To promote a golden, crispy skin on your roast duck, rub paprika over the skin before cooking. It's far easier to brown the meat this way than to risk a blackened, burned mess just for the sake of a golden glow.

When a roasted whole bird is properly cooked, the legs will move easily. Not so much that it will take off and run laps, but enough that you should be able to disjoint it by hand.

If you insist on barbequing a wild duck, you'll have far moister meat if you precook it in the oven. Remove it 20 to 30 minutes early from the oven, and then you can simply finish it on the grill to improve the appearance and add crispiness to the skin. It's really not cheating. Just don't let your guests know your secret for moist, perfectly grilled duck. Send them out for a walk or a game of badminton to build up an appetite if necessary to keep them away from the kitchen while you're doing your preliminary cooking. Then wow them as you remove your perfectly grilled ducks from the flames.

Roasting Times for Duck

Marinated duck, roasted on a rack in an uncovered pan - Cook 22 minutes per pound at 375 degrees Fahrenheit.

Unmarinated duck, roasted on a rack in an uncovered pan - Cook 30 minutes per pound at 350 degrees Fahrenheit.

The internal temperature should register 175 degrees Fahrenheit at the leg joint.

Texas Barbecued Duck

2 ducks
2 tablespoons vegetable oil

Barbecue Sauce:

2 tablespoons onion, chopped
1/4 cup butter
1/2 cup ketchup
1/2 cup lemon juice
1/4 teaspoon paprika
1/2 teaspoon salt
1/4 teaspoon pepper
1/4 teaspoon red pepper
2 tablespoons brown sugar
2 tablespoons Worcestershire sauce

To make barbecue sauce: Sauté onion in butter. Add remaining ingredients. Simmer 15 minutes.

Rub ducks with oil; brown under broiler. Brush ducks with half the barbecue sauce. Wrap each bird tightly in heavy foil, bake in shallow pan in oven at 325 degrees F for 1 hour or until tender. Remove foil last 15 minutes and spoon the remainder of barbecue sauce on the ducks. Yield: 4 servings.

NUTRITION FACTS PER SERVING: (BASED ON 1 CUP OF DUCK PER SERVING)

Nutrition Facts

Serving Size 210 g

Amount Per Serving

Calories 448 — Calories from Fat 279

	% Daily Value*
Total Fat 31.1g	**48%**
Saturated Fat 13.5g	**67%**
Trans Fat 0.0g	
Cholesterol 129mg	**43%**
Sodium 869mg	**36%**
Total Carbohydrates 14.7g	**5%**
Sugars 13.6g	
Protein 26.9g	

Vitamin A 16%   •   Vitamin C 32%
Calcium 3%   •   Iron 18%

Nutrition Grade C+

* Based on a 2000 calorie diet

Duck with Raspberry Sauce

6 duck breasts
3 tablespoons butter
3 tablespoons Framboise (raspberry brandy)
1/4 cup raspberry vinegar
3/4 cup white wine
1 tablespoon shallots, chopped
1 tablespoon beef base
1 teaspoon tomato paste
1/2 cup beef or chicken stock
1 package frozen raspberries, thawed (10 oz.)
4 kiwi fruit, peeled and sliced

Sauté the duck breasts in the butter in a skillet. Pour in the brandy and ignite carefully. Sauté until the flame subsides. Combine the vinegar, wine and shallots in a small saucepan. Cook over high heat to reduce by half. Add the beef base, tomato paste, and the beef or chicken stock. Add the sauce to the breasts and cook over low heat for 15 to 20 minutes. Puree the raspberries and sieve, discarding the seeds. To serve, add a few tablespoons of the sauce to the raspberry puree. Place the puree on a serving platter and place the breasts on the puree. Place the kiwi slices on and around the duck. Spoon the sauce over the breasts and serve immediately. Yield: 3 servings.

NUTRITION FACTS PER SERVING: (BASED ON A 6 OZ. BREAST PER SERVING)

Nutrition Facts

Serving Size 660 g

Amount Per Serving

Calories 753	Calories from Fat 250
	% Daily Value*
Total Fat 27.8g	43%
Saturated Fat 8.2g	41%
Trans Fat 0.0g	
Cholesterol 64mg	21%
Sodium 1557mg	65%
Total Carbohydrates 28.8g	10%
Dietary Fiber 9.2g	37%
Sugars 14.1g	
Protein 84.5g	
Vitamin A 11%	Vitamin C 199%
Calcium 7%	Iron 47%

Nutrition Grade D+
* Based on a 2000 calorie diet

Delicious Duck Fillet Casserole

2 wild ducks, fillets or cubes
Seasoned meat tenderizer
2 large onions, sliced
1 can cream of mushroom soup (10.5 oz.)
1 can chicken broth (14.5 oz.)
2 green peppers, sliced
1/8 teaspoon salt
1/8 teaspoon pepper
1 to 2 cups water, as needed
4 cups cooked white rice

Clean pieces of duck thoroughly under running water and pat dry. Sprinkle with tenderizer. Place onion slices under and on top of duck in a 2 1/2 quart casserole dish. Then add soup, broth and pepper slices. Sprinkle with salt and pepper and add water as needed. Bake in 350 degrees F oven 35 minutes or until done. Serve on cooked white or brown rice. Yield: 4 servings.

NUTRITION FACTS PER SERVING: (BASED ON 1 CUP OF DUCK AND RICE PER SERVING)

Nutrition Facts

Serving Size 647 g

Amount Per Serving

Calories 519	Calories from Fat 162
	% Daily Value*
Total Fat 18.0g	28%
Saturated Fat 6.0g	30%
Cholesterol 98mg	33%
Sodium 1097mg	46%
Total Carbohydrates 52.2g	17%
Dietary Fiber 2.9g	12%
Sugars 6.2g	
Protein 34.8g	

Vitamin A 7%	•	Vitamin C 89%
Calcium 7%	•	Iron 36%

Nutrition Grade B+
* Based on a 2000 calorie diet

Duck Stew

4 duck breasts
1 1/2 cups butter
2 large onions, diced
2 cans mushrooms, whole (4 oz. each)
2 cans golden mushroom soup (10.5 oz. each)

Brown duck, onion and mushrooms in butter. When brown, add enough water to cover mixture and simmer on top of stove for 1/2 hour. In casserole dish, combine mixture and golden mushroom soup and bake uncovered for 1 hour at 350 degrees F. Yield: 2 to 3 servings.

NUTRITION FACTS PER SERVING: (BASED ON A 6 OZ. DUCK BREAST PER SERVING)

Nutrition Facts

Serving Size 701 g

Amount Per Serving

Calories 1,314	Calories from Fat 1013
	% Daily Value*
Total Fat 112.6g	**173%**
Saturated Fat 61.1g	**305%**
Cholesterol 244mg	**81%**
Sodium 1942mg	**81%**
Total Carbohydrates 25.2g	**8%**
Dietary Fiber 2.5g	**10%**
Sugars 8.5g	
Protein 54.6g	
Vitamin A 58%	Vitamin C 16%
Calcium 7%	Iron 26%

Nutrition Grade C-
* Based on a 2000 calorie diet

Roasted Duck

2 ducks
6 slices bread, cubed and toasted
4 tablespoons onions, chopped
2 stalks celery with leaves, chopped
4 tablespoons slivered almonds
2 tablespoons thyme
2 tablespoons parsley
1/4 teaspoon garlic powder
4 tablespoons butter, melted
1 1/2 cups chicken broth
1 1/2 cups white wine
2 tablespoons margarine, melted
1/4 cup flour

Preheat oven to 350 degrees. Mix bread, onions, celery, almonds, thyme, parsley, garlic powder and stuff into ducks. Brush ducks with melted butter. Place in a 13 x 9" baking pan. Add wine and broth; bake, covered, at 350 degrees F for 4 hours. Mix the flour and margarine together and add to the pan juices. Stir until thick. Serve this gravy with the ducks and stuffing. Yield: 4 servings.

NUTRITION FACTS PER SERVING: (BASED ON 1 CUP OF DUCK PER SERVING)

Nutrition Facts

Serving Size 351 g

Amount Per Serving

Calories 570	Calories from Fat 303
	% Daily Value*
Total Fat 33.7g	52%
Saturated Fat 13.3g	67%
Trans Fat 0.0g	
Cholesterol 129mg	43%
Sodium 605mg	25%
Total Carbohydrates 18.9g	6%
Dietary Fiber 2.0g	8%
Sugars 2.3g	
Protein 31.4g	

Vitamin A 18%	Vitamin C 7%
Calcium 10%	Iron 36%

Nutrition Grade C
* Based on a 2000 calorie diet

Stuffed Ducks in Wine

2 ducks
1/2 cup wild rice
2 cups red wine
4 strips of bacon, chopped
1 medium onion, chopped
1/2 medium green pepper, chopped
3 celery stalks, diced
1/2 teaspoon garlic salt
1/2 teaspoon onion salt
1/4 teaspoon pepper

Cook the rice according to package. Prepare ducks for baking and marinate in wine in the refrigerator for 4 or more hours. Cook the bacon and add onion, green pepper, celery, garlic salt, onion salt and pepper; cook until the onion is tender. Add the rice to the bacon mixture. Stuff the ducks with the rice dressing mixture. Brush the ducks with softened butter. Baste the ducks with wine before cooking. Bake for 3 hours at 350 degrees, basting every half hour. Yield: 4 servings.

NUTRITION FACTS PER SERVING: (BASED ON 1 CUP OF DUCK PER SERVING)

Nutrition Facts

Serving Size 405 g

Amount Per Serving

Calories 449	Calories from Fat 146
	% Daily Value*
Total Fat 16.2g	**25%**
Saturated Fat 6.2g	**31%**
Cholesterol 106mg	**35%**
Sodium 366mg	**15%**
Total Carbohydrates 22.2g	**7%**
Dietary Fiber 2.2g	**9%**
Sugars 3.3g	
Protein 31.6g	

Vitamin A 4%	•	Vitamin C 24%
Calcium 4%	•	Iron 22%

Nutrition Grade C
* Based on a 2000 calorie diet

Duck and Potatoes

1 wild duck, cleaned
1 unpeeled apple, cut into halves
1/8 teaspoon salt
1/8 teaspoon pepper
4 large potatoes, diced
1 large onion
2 tablespoons sage

Place whole duck and apple in a 5 quart kettle with 3 to 4 cups of water; cover. Boil for 30 minutes. Discard water and apple. Add 3 to 4 cups water to parboiled duck in a baking pan; season with salt and pepper. Cover. Bake at 350 degrees F for 45 minutes. Add potatoes, onion and sage. Bake for 45 minutes to 1 hour more or until duck and potatoes are tender. If necessary, add water to keep sufficient liquid on duck and potatoes. Yield: 4 servings.

NUTRITION FACTS PER SERVING: (BASED ON 1 CUP OF DUCK PER SERVING)

Nutrition Facts

Serving Size 509 g

Amount Per Serving

Calories 408	Calories from Fat 61
	% Daily Value*
Total Fat 6.7g	10%
Saturated Fat 2.5g	12%
Trans Fat 0.0g	
Cholesterol 49mg	16%
Sodium 134mg	6%
Total Carbohydrates 68.4g	23%
Dietary Fiber 11.0g	44%
Sugars 10.6g	
Protein 19.7g	
Vitamin A 3% •	Vitamin C 130%
Calcium 7% •	Iron 21%

Nutrition Grade A
* Based on a 2000 calorie diet

Chesapeake Barbecued Duck

2 ducks
1 cup butter
1 tablespoon sugar
1 tablespoon Worcestershire sauce
1 small onion, chopped
1 teaspoon salt
1/2 cup ketchup
1 1/2 tablespoons lemon juice
1 clove garlic
1/2 teaspoon Tabasco sauce
Pepper to taste

Mix all ingredients except the ducks and simmer covered for 5 minutes. Split 2 ducks in half and flatten with meat mallet. Place on rack in flat baking pan and bake at 375 degrees F for 1 hour. Baste every 10 minutes with the sauce. Turn and cook on other side for 1 hour. Continue basting. Yield: 4 servings.

NUTRITION FACTS PER SERVING: (BASED ON 1 CUP OF DUCK PER SERVING)

Nutrition Facts

Serving Size 230 g

Amount Per Serving

Calories 684 — Calories from Fat 527

	% Daily Value*
Total Fat 58.6g	**90%**
Saturated Fat 33.8g	**169%**
Trans Fat 0.0g	
Cholesterol 220mg	**73%**
Sodium 1361mg	**57%**
Total Carbohydrates 13.5g	**5%**
Sugars 11.6g	
Protein 27.3g	

Vitamin A 36% • Vitamin C 15%
Calcium 4% • Iron 18%

Nutrition Grade D
* Based on a 2000 calorie diet

Fresh Salsa-Raspberry for Baked Duck

3 cups fresh raspberries
2 large tomatoes, seeded
1 red onion
2/3 sweet red pepper, seeded
1/2 jalapeno pepper, seeded
1 tablespoon cilantro, chopped
1 teaspoon salt
3 tablespoons balsamic vinegar
1 pouch liquid Certo® (3 oz.)
2 packets artificial sweetener

Use all fresh ingredients. Coarsely chop the first 5 ingredients; stir in the remaining ingredients; chill at least one hour and serve on baked duck. Yield: Serves 4.

Nutrition Facts

Serving Size 245 g

Amount Per Serving

Calories 84	Calories from Fat 8
	% Daily Value*
Total Fat 0.9g	1%
Trans Fat 0.0g	
Cholesterol 0mg	0%
Sodium 589mg	25%
Total Carbohydrates 18.6g	6%
Dietary Fiber 8.0g	32%
Sugars 8.6g	
Protein 2.4g	

Vitamin A 29%	Vitamin C 107%
Calcium 4%	Iron 6%

Nutrition Grade A
* Based on a 2000 calorie diet

Duck Gumbo

2 ducks
3 tablespoons bacon drippings
3 tablespoons flour
1 onion, sliced
2 bunches green onions, sliced
1 green pepper, cubed
4 cloves garlic
2 cups okra, sliced
1 can tomatoes (20 oz.)
3 quarts water
2 bay leaves
1 1/2 teaspoons salt
1/8 teaspoon red pepper
1 lb. shrimp, cooked
1/2 pint oysters
6 oz. crabmeat

Soak ducks in a mixture of baking soda and water overnight, drain. Cook ducks in water seasoned with a little salt and pepper until meat is very tender. Remove meat from bones.

Make a very dark roux of flour and bacon drippings. Set aside. Cover and steam onions, peppers and garlic and okra in a large Dutch oven. When just about done, add tomatoes and cook until almost brown. Add water, bay leaves, salt and pepper. Stir in cooked shrimp, roux and duck meat. Cover and cook slowly for 1 hour. Add oysters and crabmeat and cook for an additional 15 minutes. Serve in soup plates with rice in bottom. Yield: Serves 6.

NUTRITION FACTS PER SERVING: (BASED ON 1 CUP OF DUCK PER SERVING, NO RICE INCLUDED)

Nutrition Facts

Serving Size 1117 g

Amount Per Serving

Calories 501	Calories from Fat 167
	% Daily Value*
Total Fat 18.6g	**29%**
Saturated Fat 5.3g	**27%**
Cholesterol 252mg	**84%**
Sodium 1599mg	**67%**
Total Carbohydrates 40.5g	**14%**
Dietary Fiber 8.6g	**34%**
Sugars 3.6g	
Protein 46.8g	

Vitamin A 59%	•	Vitamin C 97%
Calcium 27%	•	Iron 57%

Nutrition Grade A

* Based on a 2000 calorie diet

Saucy Duck with Dressing

8 boneless breast halves (duck or pheasant)
1 lb. breakfast sausage
1/2 onion, diced
1/2 green pepper, diced
1 cup wild rice
3 cups bread cubes
1/2 cup chicken broth
8 slices bacon

Mushroom Sauce:

1/2 cup mushrooms, sliced
1/4 cup butter
1/4 cup flour
1/4 teaspoon white pepper
3/4 cup chicken broth
1/2 cup half & half

Prepare dressing by browning sausage, green pepper and onion; drain fat. Cook rice according to package instructions. Combine broth and bread cubes and mix until moist, then add rice and sausage mixture; mix well. Put one-fourth of dressing mixture on top of each of 4 breast halves. Add the remaining 4 breast halves on top of the dressing. Wrap each breast combo with 2 slices bacon and hold together with toothpicks. Place in an 8 inch covered baking dish and bake at 350 degrees F for 45 minutes. Remove cover and bake until browned. During final baking, sauté mushrooms in butter. Stir in flour and pepper, then blend in broth and half & half. Cook until thickened. When breasts are done, remove toothpicks and cover with mushroom sauce. Yield: Serves 4.

NUTRITION FACTS PER SERVING: (BASED ON A 6 OZ. DUCK BREAST PER SERVING)

Nutrition Facts

Serving Size 674 g

Amount Per Serving

Calories 1,284   Calories from Fat 602

	% Daily Value*
Total Fat 66.9g	**103%**
Saturated Fat 22.0g	**110%**
Trans Fat 0.3g	
Cholesterol 153mg	**51%**
Sodium 1666mg	**69%**
Total Carbohydrates 55.0g	**18%**
Dietary Fiber 3.3g	**13%**
Sugars 2.4g	
Protein 107.5g	

Vitamin A 12%   •   Vitamin C 24%
Calcium 13%   •   Iron 25%

Nutrition Grade C

* Based on a 2000 calorie diet

Hunter's Booya

4 wild ducks – cleaned and halved
6 lbs. venison
2 lbs. pork, cubed
2 soup bones, 1/2 lb. each
4 large onions, sliced
2 cups parsley sprigs
1/2 cup dry split peas
1/2 cup dry lima beans
1/4 cup salt
2 tablespoons pepper
2 tablespoons garlic salt
1 tablespoon basil
1 tablespoon oregano
1 teaspoon thyme

In a very large kettle, combine meat, ducks, soup bones, onions, parsley, split peas, lima beans and seasonings. Add water to cover. Bring to a boil. Reduce heat, cover, and simmer 4 to 5 hours or until meat is tender. Remove meat from bones and cube. Discard bones, skim fat from stock and return meat to kettle.

Add:

3 cups diced carrots
3 cups diced celery
1 large head red cabbage, coarsely chopped
3 cups diced rutabaga
1 cup diced green pepper

Simmer covered for 1 hour.

Add:

3 cans tomatoes, undrained (28 oz. each)
3 cans cut green beans, undrained (15 1/2 oz. each)
2 pkg. frozen peas (10 oz. each)
2 pkg. frozen whole kernel corn (10 oz. each)

Simmer covered 1 hour more. Yield: Serves 30.

NUTRITION FACTS PER SERVING: (BASED ON 1 CUP OF DUCK PER SERVING)

Nutrition Facts

Serving Size 395 g

Amount Per Serving

Calories 296	Calories from Fat 51

	% Daily Value*
Total Fat 5.7g	9%
Saturated Fat 1.7g	8%
Trans Fat 0.0g	
Cholesterol 48mg	16%
Sodium 1337mg	56%
Total Carbohydrates 20.6g	7%
Dietary Fiber 6.0g	24%
Sugars 8.1g	
Protein 39.4g	

Vitamin A 63%	•	Vitamin C 47%
Calcium 7%	•	Iron 18%

Nutrition Grade A

* Based on a 2000 calorie diet

Sweet and Sour Duck

2 wild ducks, dressed and cut into pieces, breasts cut into at least 2 pieces
2 tablespoons margarine
2 cups sauerkraut
1 can orange juice concentrate (6 oz.)
1/4 cup water
1/2 teaspoon caraway seeds

Melt margarine in large heavy skillet and brown all pieces of duck. Put duck pieces in large casserole dish. Scatter sauerkraut over duck. Combine orange juice concentrate with 1/4 cup water and caraway seeds. Pour over sauerkraut. Tightly cover casserole dish. Bake at 325 degrees F for 1 to 1 1/2 hours or until duck is tender. Yield: Serves 4.

NUTRITION FACTS PER SERVING: (BASED ON 1 CUP OF DUCK PER SERVING)

Nutrition Facts

Serving Size 231 g

Amount Per Serving

Calories 306 Calories from Fat 164

	% Daily Value*
Total Fat 18.3g	28%
Saturated Fat 5.6g	28%
Cholesterol 98mg	33%
Sodium 608mg	25%
Total Carbohydrates 7.6g	3%
Dietary Fiber 2.2g	9%
Sugars 1.3g	
Protein 27.0g	

Vitamin A 8%	Vitamin C 41%
Calcium 4%	Iron 23%

Nutrition Grade B
* Based on a 2000 calorie diet

Orange Wild Duck

4 ducks
1/4 teaspoon salt
1/8 teaspoon pepper
2 apples, cut up
2 onions, cut up
2 celery stalks, cut up
6 slices of bacon
1 cup of orange juice
Orange slices for garnish

Rub the ducks inside and out with salt and pepper. Stuff the ducks with cut up pieces of apple, onion and celery. Cover the breasts with strips of bacon, place in a roaster pan. Cook in oven at 375 degrees F. When the ducks begin to brown, pour 2 to 3 cups of boiling water around them, reduce the heat to 325 degrees F.

Roast for at least 3 hours, basting every 15 to 20 minutes and also keep skimming off the excess fat. During the last half hour, add 1 cup of orange juice - pour it over the ducks and baste at least once with the juice added to the water. Serve with garnishes of orange slices. Yield: 4 servings.

NUTRITION FACTS PER SERVING: (BASED ON 1 CUP OF DUCK PER SERVING)

Nutrition Facts

Serving Size 459 g

Amount Per Serving

Calories 600	Calories from Fat 260
	% Daily Value*
Total Fat 28.9g	44%
Saturated Fat 10.6g	53%
Trans Fat 0.0g	
Cholesterol 207mg	69%
Sodium 521mg	22%
Total Carbohydrates 26.0g	9%
Dietary Fiber 3.7g	15%
Sugars 18.2g	
Protein 56.6g	
Vitamin A 8%	Vitamin C 76%
Calcium 6%	Iron 36%

Nutrition Grade B

* Based on a 2000 calorie diet

Roast Duck with Potato Dressing

4 to 5 lb. duckling
1 onion, chopped
4 tablespoons butter
3/4 cup dry bread crumbs
1 cup mashed potatoes
1 egg
1 1/2 teaspoons salt
1/2 teaspoon pepper

Prepare duck for baking. Sauté onion in butter. Mix the butter, bread crumbs, potatoes, egg, salt and pepper together and combine with onion. Stuff duck lightly. Roast duck in a 350 degree F oven for 1 hour, uncovered. After an hour, cover the bird and roast for another hour. Yield: 2 servings.

NUTRITION FACTS PER SERVING: (BASED ON 1 CUP OF DUCK PER SERVING)

Nutrition Facts

Serving Size 383 g

Amount Per Serving

Calories 741 — Calories from Fat 372

	% Daily Value*
Total Fat 41.3g	**64%**
Saturated Fat 21.0g	**105%**
Cholesterol 244mg	**81%**
Sodium 2584mg	**108%**
Total Carbohydrates 54.4g	**18%**
Dietary Fiber 2.9g	**12%**
Sugars 5.0g	
Protein 37.8g	

Vitamin A 19%	•	Vitamin C 8%
Calcium 15%	•	Iron 34%

Nutrition Grade D+
* Based on a 2000 calorie diet

PHEASANT RECIPES

Pheasant

Tips for Cooking Pheasant

Pheasants are relative newcomers in North America, since they immigrated just over 130 years ago from Asia. The little creatures found it quite pleasant here and have since flourished throughout most of the United States. If you're bringing home some of these tasty morsels this hunting season, you'll find many flavorful and easy ways to prepare and serve them.

Pheasants have a delicate, earthy flavor and are only mildly gamey, as they dine mainly on grass and seeds. Recipes for chicken and rabbit are usually good contenders for pheasant preparation, but we've found some great recipes that will bring out the subtle, delicious flavors of wild pheasant.

Pheasant has 133 calories in a 3.5 ounce portion of skinless meat. It's rich in vitamin B6 and iron, and it has a significant amount of potassium. That 3.5 ounce piece of meat has 3.6 grams of fat, but if you leave the skin on the fat content jumps up to 9.3 grams.

Smoking Pheasant

Smoked pheasant can be a gourmet delight or chew sticks for your dog. It's all in the preparation, but if you're patient, it's a simple and delicious way to prepare your bird.

Wild pheasants work hard for a living, so their flesh is naturally tough. To minimize the effects of their hard lifestyle, you must brine the meat to tenderize it. Brining can take as much as 12 hours to fully tenderize the meat and if you short-change the process, you'll wind up with a tough piece of flesh you dog will just love.

Two pheasants will serve four hungry or six waif-like guests, so adjust the recipe according to the number you'll be feeding.

Since the meat needs to soak in brine for at least 12 hours, this is a two-day process.

Your ingredients are as follows:

2 whole pheasants
1/4 cup kosher salt
1/4 cup brown sugar
2 cups maple syrup, reduced to one cup
4 cups water

Use a lidded container that will just fit the two birds. Add the salt, brown sugar, and water to the container and submerge the birds. Cover and place in the refrigerator for 12 to 18 hours.

Remove birds from water and pat dry. Place them on a cooling rack under a fan or in a breeze for one to three hours to let them dry. This is important for the smoking process to work well.

In a medium saucepan over medium-high heat, reduce maple syrup down to one cup, 5 to 10 minutes.

Smoke the pheasants with the wood of your choice in a 200 to 250 degree Fahrenheit smoker. This will take from three to five hours. After one hour of smoking, baste the meat with the maple syrup reduction. Baste every thirty minutes thereafter.

When the thigh meat reaches an internal temperature of 160 degrees Fahrenheit, remove the meat from the smoker. Place the birds on a cooling rack and baste with the maple syrup. Let rest 20 minutes before serving. This may be served hot or cold.

General Cooking Tips

Because of their delicate size and structure, you can clip off the feet and wings of your pheasant with sturdy kitchen shears.

A week or two in the freezer will help to tenderize pheasant meat.

It's best to cook pheasant for a longer period at a lower temperature. 275 degrees Fahrenheit is sufficient for roasting, or place the bird on an upper rack for grilling.

Baste pheasant frequently to preserve moisture in the meat. Melted butter blended with your favorite herbs and spices makes a good basting mixture.

Since pheasant's flavor has an earthy undertone, it pairs perfectly with mushroom and garlic. Sweet and fruity glazes are also well suited for this flavorful bird.

Braising, grilling or moist preparations are favored for pheasant and smoked pheasant is a gourmet treat.

Hanging pheasant for several days will tenderize the meat. Cool temperatures of less than 50 degrees Fahrenheit must be maintained to prevent bacteria growth. Feathers should be left intact to keep the skin supple.

Brining your pheasant reduces any gamey flavor and helps to hold in moisture when the meat is cooked.

Wild pheasant will be drier than domestic pheasant, and since they aren't pampered in feed lots, they may be tougher than their domesticated cousins. The breast of a wild pheasant will be the tenderest portion of the bird. Often, the legs, thighs and wings are used for stock, stew or cooked in a slow cooker.

If you have a young bird and want to roast or grill it, cook it until it is rare. A thermometer inserted in the meatiest portion of the bird should read 140 degrees Fahrenheit for a perfectly done rare pheasant.

To help keep your pheasant moist, use the Beer Can method of cookery. Open a can of beer and place it upright inside the cavity of the bird. Stand it in an oven-proof dish and bake. The liquid steams the bird from the inside as it roasts from the outside.

Cook your pheasant with a turkey roasting bag to lock in all the juices.

Breast meat cooks more quickly than the thighs and legs get tender. When the breast is done, take the bird from the pan and separate the breast. Remove the leg quarters and place them back into the pan with its juices. Cover and cook for an additional 30 to 60 minutes or until the meat falls off the bone. Keep the breast meat warm and covered. If necessary, reheat the meat before serving.

Dakota Pheasant

1/2 cup margarine
1 pheasant (cut up for frying)
1 cup flour
1/8 teaspoon salt
1/8 teaspoon pepper
1 cup whipping cream
1/2 cup sour cream

Melt margarine in frying pan. Combine flour, salt and pepper and dredge pheasant pieces in flour mixture. Fry until golden brown. Remove pieces from pan and put in casserole dish. Add sweet cream and sour cream to drippings and heat. Pour over pheasant. Cover and bake for 1 1/2 hours at 350 degrees F. Yield: 3 servings.

Nutrition Facts

Serving Size 302 g

Amount Per Serving

Calories 722	Calories from Fat 413
	% Daily Value*
Total Fat 45.9g	**71%**
Saturated Fat 11.9g	**59%**
Cholesterol 124mg	**41%**
Sodium 529mg	**22%**
Total Carbohydrates 33.8g	**11%**
Dietary Fiber 1.1g	**5%**
Protein 41.5g	

Vitamin A 38%	•	Vitamin C 16%
Calcium 8%	•	Iron 21%

Nutrition Grade B

* Based on a 2000 calorie diet

Kraut Pheasant with Apple

1 pheasant, cleaned, rinsed & drained well
1 teaspoon salt
2 tablespoons butter
1 1/2 tablespoons flour
3 cups sauerkraut
2 tablespoons brown sugar
2 medium tart apples, peeled
1/4 cup water
4 teaspoons white wine
1/2 teaspoon caraway seeds

Cut pheasant into pieces and sprinkle with salt. Brown slowly on all sides in butter in a skillet. Remove pheasant from the pan and stir the flour into drippings in pan. Add brown sugar and sauerkraut; mix to blend thoroughly. Turn into a 2 1/2 quart casserole dish. Arrange the browned pheasant on top of sauerkraut. Cut the apple into chunks and arrange on top of pheasant. Add the water; cover and bake at 350 degrees F for 45 minutes. Sprinkle with wine and caraway seeds; cover and bake for 25 to 30 more minutes. Yield: 4 servings.

Nutrition Facts

Serving Size 322 g

Amount Per Serving

Calories 268	Calories from Fat 83
	% Daily Value*
Total Fat 9.2g	**14%**
Saturated Fat 4.8g	**24%**
Trans Fat 0.0g	
Cholesterol 73mg	**24%**
Sodium 1362mg	**57%**
Total Carbohydrates 24.0g	**8%**
Dietary Fiber 5.4g	**22%**
Sugars 15.8g	
Protein 22.1g	

| Vitamin A 8% | • | Vitamin C 42% |
| Calcium 6% | • | Iron 16% |

Nutrition Grade C

* Based on a 2000 calorie diet

Pheasant Supreme

4 pheasant breasts
1/2 cup margarine
1 can cream of mushroom soup, reduced sodium (10.5 oz.)
1 can cream of chicken soup (10.5 oz.)
1 can chicken with rice soup (10.5 oz.)
1 cup sliced fresh mushrooms
1 teaspoon garlic flakes
1 tablespoon onion flakes
1/4 cup dry wine (red or white, optional)
1/2 cup flour
1/8 teaspoon salt
1/8 teaspoon pepper

Cut pheasants into 1/4 inch thick pieces. Roll pheasant pieces in flour. Sauté in margarine using a deep skillet on medium heat for approximately 20 to 30 minutes. Season with salt and pepper. Add remaining ingredients and simmer, covered, over low heat for 1 hour or until pheasant is tender. Serve over mashed potatoes, rice or noodles. Yield: 4 servings.

Nutrition Facts

Serving Size 654 g

Amount Per Serving

Calories 893	Calories from Fat 382
	% Daily Value*
Total Fat 42.4g	**65%**
Saturated Fat 10.0g	**50%**
Cholesterol 244mg	**81%**
Sodium 1740mg	**72%**
Total Carbohydrates 30.5g	**10%**
Dietary Fiber 1.6g	**7%**
Sugars 3.2g	
Protein 90.5g	
Vitamin A 40%	Vitamin C 38%
Calcium 9%	Iron 39%

Nutrition Grade C

* Based on a 2000 calorie diet

Wild Rice and Pheasant

1 cup uncooked wild rice
3 cups water
2 cups cooked pheasant
1/3 cup onion, chopped
1/4 cup butter
1/3 cup flour
1 teaspoon salt
1/8 teaspoon pepper
1 cup half and half
1 cup pheasant stock or chicken broth
1 can mushrooms (4 oz.)
1 can water chestnuts (8 oz.)

Wash the wild rice. Bring the 3 cups of water to a boil in saucepan, then add rice. Return water to a boil and stir. Reduce heat; cover and simmer 45 minutes or until rice kernels puff open. Fluff rice and simmer 5 more minutes. Drain excess liquid.

Cut cooked pheasant into bite size pieces. In a pan, sauté 1/3 cup chopped onion and 1/4 cup butter. Blend in 1/3 cup flour, salt, and pepper. Gradually stir in 1 cup half & half and 1 cup pheasant stock. Cook until thickened. Mix sauce, pheasant, water chestnuts, and mushrooms into cooked rice. Bake in 2 quart casserole for 30 minutes at 425 degrees F. Yield: 6 servings.

Nutrition Facts

Serving Size 367 g

Amount Per Serving

Calories 406 — Calories from Fat 155

	% Daily Value*
Total Fat 17.2g	26%
Saturated Fat 9.3g	47%
Cholesterol 113mg	38%
Sodium 635mg	26%
Total Carbohydrates 27.8g	9%
Dietary Fiber 2.0g	8%
Sugars 1.1g	
Protein 34.4g	

Vitamin A 12% • Vitamin C 13%
Calcium 7% • Iron 13%

Nutrition Grade B-
* Based on a 2000 calorie diet

Grilled Marinated Pheasant

1 cup vegetable oil
1 cup soy sauce
1/2 cup lemon juice
1 medium onion, minced
1 teaspoon ginger
1/4 teaspoon garlic powder
4 full pheasant breasts

Combine all ingredients in shallow pan for marinating overnight or for several hours. Reserve 1/2 cup of marinade for basting while grilling. Cover and refrigerate, turning breasts over once while marinating. Grill on a gas grill for approximately 40 minutes, turning at least once and basting periodically. Charcoal grill will take a little longer. Yield: 4 servings.

NUTRITION FACTS PER SERVING: (BASED ON USING ONLY THE 1/2 CUP OF BASTING MARINADE PER SERVING)

Nutrition Facts

Serving Size 396 g

Amount Per Serving

Calories 602	Calories from Fat 239
	% Daily Value*
Total Fat 26.5g	41%
Saturated Fat 7.1g	35%
Cholesterol 232mg	77%
Sodium 1031mg	43%
Total Carbohydrates 2.0g	1%
Sugars 0.7g	
Protein 84.1g	

Vitamin A 12%	•	Vitamin C 42%
Calcium 5%	•	Iron 24%

Nutrition Grade B
* Based on a 2000 calorie diet

Fargo Pheasant Stew

1 pheasant, cut into serving pieces
Flour for dredging
1/8 teaspoon salt
1/8 teaspoon pepper
4 tablespoons butter
1/3 cup onion, chopped
1/3 cup celery, chopped
1/3 cup carrot, chopped
2 bay leaves
1/2 cup dry white wine
1 cup chicken stock

Preheat the oven to 250 degrees F. Dredge the pheasant in the flour seasoned with salt and pepper. Brown the pheasant in butter in a skillet, then remove to a roasting pan. Add the onion, celery, carrot, bay leaves, wine and chicken stock to the pan. Cover and bake at 250 degrees F for 5 1/2 to 6 hours. Yield: Serves 3.

Nutrition Facts

Serving Size 299 g

Amount Per Serving

Calories 352	Calories from Fat 180
	% Daily Value*
Total Fat 20.0g	**31%**
Saturated Fat 11.3g	**56%**
Trans Fat 0.0g	
Cholesterol 118mg	**39%**
Sodium 526mg	**22%**
Total Carbohydrates 6.6g	**2%**
Dietary Fiber 1.0g	**4%**
Sugars 1.9g	
Protein 28.7g	
Vitamin A 56% •	Vitamin C 16%
Calcium 5% •	Iron 11%

Nutrition Grade C-

* Based on a 2000 calorie diet

Baked Pheasant in Cream

1 pheasant, cut up
2 cups flour
1 teaspoon salt
1 teaspoon pepper
4 tablespoons butter
1 pint half and half cream

Place cut up pheasant in brown bag with flour, salt and pepper. Shake to coat each piece well. Brown pheasant pieces in butter in frying pan. Place browned pheasant in small roasting pan; cover with cream. Bake at 350 degrees F until cream bubbles; then turn down to 325 degrees F. Bake for 1 hour. Yield: 3 to 4 servings.

Nutrition Facts

Serving Size 287 g

Amount Per Serving

Calories 604	Calories from Fat 262
	% Daily Value*
Total Fat 29.1g	45%
Saturated Fat 17.1g	85%
Cholesterol 133mg	44%
Sodium 746mg	31%
Total Carbohydrates 53.2g	18%
Dietary Fiber 1.8g	7%
Protein 30.9g	

Vitamin A 19%	Vitamin C 11%
Calcium 15%	Iron 23%

Nutrition Grade B
* Based on a 2000 calorie diet

Braised Slow Cooker Pheasant

2 pheasants, 1.5 lbs. each or 1 pheasant, 3 lbs. split
1/8 teaspoon salt
1/8 teaspoon pepper
2 carrots, pared and quartered
1 onion, sliced
2 slices bacon
1/4 cup dry sherry or broth
1/4 cup chicken broth

Sprinkle the cavity of each pheasant sparingly with salt and pepper. Put the carrots and onions in a slow cooker. Add the pheasants on top of vegetables. Chop bacon slices into pieces and place over each breast. Add sherry and broth to slow cooker. Cook, covered, on low for 8 to 10 hours (or on high for 2 1/2 to 3 1/2 hours). Yield: 4 servings.

Nutrition Facts

Serving Size 269 g

Amount Per Serving

Calories 303	Calories from Fat 77
	% Daily Value*
Total Fat 8.6g	**13%**
Saturated Fat 2.9g	**14%**
Trans Fat 0.0g	
Cholesterol 121mg	**40%**
Sodium 318mg	**13%**
Total Carbohydrates 5.8g	**2%**
Dietary Fiber 1.3g	**5%**
Sugars 2.7g	
Protein 44.1g	

Vitamin A 108%	•	Vitamin C 24%
Calcium 4%	•	Iron 13%

Nutrition Grade A-
* Based on a 2000 calorie diet

Pheasant in Green Peppercorn Sauce

4 tablespoons butter
1 pheasant, quartered
2 tablespoons onion, minced
1/2 cup dry white wine
4 teaspoons green peppercorns, rinsed and drained
1 cup heavy cream
1/2 teaspoon dried tarragon
Salt and black pepper to taste

Melt the butter in a skillet on medium-high heat. Add the pheasant and sauté until golden. Cover and cook over low heat for 30 minutes, or until tender. Remove to a plate and keep warm.

Add the onion to the skillet and sauté over low heat until limp. Add the wine. Increase the heat and boil until the wine is reduced by half, scraping up any brown bits of pheasant. Mash 2 teaspoons of the peppercorns, leaving the remainder whole. Stir the cream, mashed and whole peppercorns, and tarragon into the skillet. Continue boiling until the sauce is syrupy. Remove from heat and season with salt and pepper to taste. Pour the sauce over the pheasant and serve. Yield: Serves 3.

Nutrition Facts

Serving Size 225 g

Amount Per Serving

Calories 473	Calories from Fat 311
	% Daily Value*
Total Fat 34.5g	53%
Saturated Fat 20.4g	102%
Cholesterol 173mg	58%
Sodium 171mg	7%
Total Carbohydrates 4.7g	2%
Dietary Fiber 0.9g	3%
Sugars 0.7g	
Protein 29.1g	
Vitamin A 25%	Vitamin C 14%
Calcium 6%	Iron 13%

Nutrition Grade C
* Based on a 2000 calorie diet

Pheasant with Stuffing

3 pheasant breasts, cubed
1 can cream of mushroom soup (10.5 oz.)
Sour cream (8 oz.)
1 cup Swiss cheese
3/4 cup chicken broth
1/4 cup margarine, melted
1 cup Pepperidge Farm® stuffing

Heat cream of mushroom soup and sour cream. Place pheasant in a greased baking dish. Pour soup mixture over pheasant. Top with Swiss cheese. Bake at 350 degrees F uncovered for 50 minutes. Then heat the broth and melted margarine in a pan until hot. Mix the stuffing mix with broth mixture. Sprinkle over pheasant and cook for 10 more minutes. Yield: 3 servings.

(Note: Using a low sodium cream of mushroom soup and less margarine will lower the sodium content.)

Nutrition Facts

Serving Size 675 g

Amount Per Serving

Calories 1,050 — Calories from Fat 538

	% Daily Value*
Total Fat 59.8g	**92%**
Saturated Fat 24.3g	**122%**
Trans Fat 0.0g	
Cholesterol 319mg	**106%**
Sodium 1427mg	**59%**
Total Carbohydrates 19.3g	**6%**
Sugars 5.4g	
Protein 99.6g	

Vitamin A 42% • Vitamin C 35%
Calcium 41% • Iron 32%

Nutrition Grade B-
* Based on a 2000 calorie diet

Pheasant Pie

1 pheasant, 2 lbs.
1 stalk celery
1 bay leaf
6 peppercorns
1 tablespoon salt
1/2 cup margarine
5 tablespoons flour
1 cup cream
1/8 teaspoon black pepper
1/8 teaspoon salt
24 small whole white onions, parboiled
1/4 lb. mushrooms, sliced
2 cups cooked fresh peas, or 1 pkg. frozen, thawed
1 unbaked pie crust to cover casserole

Rinse bird and place in large pot with water to cover. Add celery, bay leaf, peppercorns and 1 tablespoon salt. Cover and simmer over low heat until bird is tender and meat falls from bone - about 2 hours. Remove meat and set aside. Strain 1 pint of liquid and reserve.

Melt margarine in a saucepan and blend in the flour. Gradually add the reserved liquid, stirring. Add the cream, salt and pepper. Cook over medium heat, stirring constantly until thickened. Place meat in a 2 quart casserole and add onions, mushrooms and peas. Pour sauce over all, leaving 1" space at top. Place pastry over casserole. Bake at 450 degrees F for 15 to 20 minutes or until crust is golden. Yield: Serves 4.

NUTRITION FACTS PER SERVING: (CALCULATED USING FRESH PEAS AS OPPOSED TO FROZEN)

Nutrition Facts

Serving Size 576 g

Amount Per Serving

Calories 928	Calories from Fat 449
	% Daily Value*
Total Fat 49.9g	**77%**
Saturated Fat 12.5g	**62%**
Cholesterol 161mg	**54%**
Sodium 2435mg	**101%**
Total Carbohydrates 54.8g	**18%**
Dietary Fiber 8.4g	**34%**
Sugars 11.8g	
Protein 64.4g	

| Vitamin A 42% | • | Vitamin C 90% |
| Calcium 11% | • | Iron 37% |

Nutrition Grade B

* Based on a 2000 calorie diet

Pheasant in Mushroom Sauce

3 lbs. pheasant, cut in pieces
1/4 cup flour
1/4 cup butter, melted
8 small onions, boiled
1/4 lb. sliced mushrooms
1 cup grated processed cheese
1 can cream mushroom soup (10.5 oz.)
1 can nonfat evaporated milk (12 oz.)
1/2 teaspoon salt
1/8 teaspoon pepper

Coat pheasant pieces with flour and place pieces in single layer in melted butter in shallow 9 x 13 inch baking dish. Bake uncovered at 425 degrees F for 30 minutes. Turn pheasant and bake 30 minutes more. Pour off excess fat and add onions and mushrooms to pheasant. Mix cheese, soup, milk, salt and pepper and pour over pheasant. Cover dish with aluminum foil. Reduce heat to 325 degrees F and bake 30 minutes more. Yield: Serves 6.

Nutrition Facts

Serving Size 479 g

Amount Per Serving

Calories 578	Calories from Fat 215
	% Daily Value*
Total Fat 23.9g	**37%**
Saturated Fat 11.3g	**56%**
Cholesterol 187mg	**62%**
Sodium 961mg	**40%**
Total Carbohydrates 24.6g	**8%**
Dietary Fiber 1.9g	**8%**
Sugars 12.9g	
Protein 64.2g	
Vitamin A 20% •	Vitamin C 36%
Calcium 33% •	Iron 25%

Nutrition Grade B
* Based on a 2000 calorie diet

Cheesy Pheasant Casserole

4 pheasant breasts
3 eggs, beaten
1 can mushroom soup (10.5 oz.)
1 onion, chopped
3 cups chicken breast, chopped
1 1/2 cups grated American cheese
3 cups Ritz crackers, crushed
1 teaspoon pepper

Simmer pheasant in water to cover and remove meat from bones. Mix together all the rest of the ingredients. Add chopped pheasant. Place mixture in 9 x 13-inch baking pan. Bake 1 hour and 15 minutes at 350 degrees F. Yield: 5 servings.

Nutrition Facts

Serving Size 650 g

Amount Per Serving

Calories 1,444	Calories from Fat 614
	% Daily Value*
Total Fat 68.2g	**105%**
Saturated Fat 19.0g	**95%**
Trans Fat 0.0g	
Cholesterol 388mg	**129%**
Sodium 2246mg	**94%**
Total Carbohydrates 98.2g	**33%**
Sugars 13.4g	
Protein 106.1g	
Vitamin A 17% •	Vitamin C 31%
Calcium 45% •	Iron 51%

Nutrition Grade C+

* Based on a 2000 calorie diet

Pheasant a la Silvio

2 pheasants
1/2 teaspoon oregano
1/2 teaspoon thyme
1/8 teaspoon salt
1/8 teaspoon pepper
1 garlic clove, chopped
1 cup flour
4 tablespoons butter
3 bacon slices, cut into 1/2 -inch pieces
2 tablespoons butter
2 onions, chopped
1/2 lb. shallots, diced
1/2 lb. mushrooms, chopped
1 cup burgundy wine
1/2 cup chicken broth
1 tablespoon cornstarch

Cut pheasants into portion-size pieces. Put oregano, thyme, salt, pepper and garlic into large paper bag with enough flour to coat pheasant pieces and shake well. Brown the pheasant in butter in a skillet. Remove from butter and bake at 350 degrees F for 1 hour.

Cook bacon and set aside. Sauté onions and shallots in butter, just until transparent. Then add bacon, mushrooms, wine and chicken stock. Simmer. Put baked pheasant in sauce, add cornstarch for desired thickness. Simmer 15 to 20 minutes or until done. Yield: 4 servings.

Nutrition Facts

Serving Size 494 g

Amount Per Serving

Calories 665	Calories from Fat 238

	% Daily Value*
Total Fat 26.5g	**41%**
Saturated Fat 13.9g	**70%**
Trans Fat 0.0g	
Cholesterol 167mg	**56%**
Sodium 483mg	**20%**
Total Carbohydrates 44.5g	**15%**
Dietary Fiber 2.5g	**10%**
Sugars 4.0g	
Protein 51.2g	

Vitamin A 30%	Vitamin C 35%
Calcium 8%	Iron 36%

Nutrition Grade C

* Based on a 2000 calorie diet

Pheasant Mushroom Casserole

4 pheasants, boned
1 cup flour
1/8 teaspoon salt
1/8 teaspoon pepper
1/2 teaspoon poultry seasoning
4 tablespoons butter
2 cans cream of mushroom soup (10.5 oz. each)
2 cans mushrooms, (4 oz. each)
1 onion, minced
1/2 cup dry white wine

Remove meat from bones and shake the pieces in flour, seasoned with salt, pepper, and poultry seasoning. Brown the pieces quickly in a pan with butter, then arrange them in a greased casserole. Combine the soup, mushrooms (with their juice), onion, and wine. Pour over the meat. Cover and bake at 350 degrees F for 1 hour. Yield: 4 servings.

Nutrition Facts

Serving Size 660 g

Amount Per Serving

Calories 798	Calories from Fat 261

	% Daily Value*
Total Fat 29.0g	45%
Saturated Fat 12.7g	64%
Cholesterol 263mg	88%
Sodium 912mg	38%
Total Carbohydrates 35.0g	12%
Dietary Fiber 2.3g	9%
Sugars 2.6g	
Protein 89.2g	

Vitamin A 19%	•	Vitamin C 39%
Calcium 8%	•	Iron 36%

Nutrition Grade C-

* Based on a 2000 calorie diet

RABBIT RECIPES

Rabbit

Tips for Cooking Rabbit

Did you know that rabbit is lower in cholesterol than turkey or chicken and has a mere 795 calories per pound? It has the lowest percentage of fat and the highest percentage of protein of any meat. It's a meat that's healthy, delicious and can be prepared in many ways to please every palate.

Tame or Wild Rabbit

If you've had a bit of bad luck while hunting, you can purchase tame rabbit to use in any of the recipes we're featuring. Domestic rabbit is ready to pop in the pan as soon as you bring it home. However, if your aim has been good and you come home with wild rabbit, it may have a slightly gamey taste. It's also leaner than tame rabbit.

You can minimize the taste by soaking the meat in salty water overnight. Just like any meat, a young animal will be tenderer and have a more delicate flavor, so your cooking method may change depending on the age of your rabbit. A few tablespoons of salt should do to draw the blood out of the meat.

Age and Size of Your Rabbit

A young rabbit is usually weighs between one and three pounds. The flesh is pink and fine-grained. The meat is tender and may be prepared just like poultry. These smaller, young rabbits are known as "fryers."

An older rabbit is known as a "roaster." They are over eight months old and have a darker, coarse-grained flesh. This meat can be tough, so slow, moist cooking like stewing or braising will help tenderize the flesh and give you far more palatable results.

General Cooking Tips for Rabbit

For safety, the internal temperature of rabbit should reach 160 degrees Fahrenheit.

Bones help to lock in moisture, so you shouldn't debone the meat before cooking. Since rabbit is a very lean meat, it can easily dry out and become tough.

Don't overcook the meat when frying or searing. It will toughen and dry out the flesh. However, if you are using a liquid in a slow cooker, poaching or braising, slow cooking at a low temperature will tenderize the meat.

Braising

When you braise, you're searing the meat quickly at a high temperature to seal in the juices. Use a heavy skillet with a tight-fitting lid. Rub the meat with olive or canola oil and place in a preheated pan. Once the meat is brown on all sides, add liquid to the pan, cover and simmer slowly.

Roasting

If you have a young rabbit, it can be roasted just like chicken. Rub the parts with olive or canola oil, and add your favorite herbs, vegetables and seasonings. Roast at 350 degrees until internal temperature reads 160 degrees Fahrenheit.

Stewing

Slow stewing tenderizes the meat and allows your seasonings and herbs to permeate the flesh. Flour and quickly brown the meat in olive or canola oil. Add liquid such as water, stock and wine. Add seasonings and simmer on a very low heat for at least two hours. Add vegetables the last hour of cooking.

Sautéing and Frying

Thin cuts of rabbit that are less than one inch thick can be sautéed. If the meat is from an older animal, pound the flesh with a mallet to tenderize it. You may dredge the pieces in flour or cook them without any coating.

Preheat a skillet, add a little oil and brown the meat on both sides until it reaches 160 degrees Fahrenheit.

Frying merely requires more oil than sautéing. Frying will give the outer layer a crispy crust, so coating your meat with flour or crumbs is preferable to hold in the juices.

Herbs and Spices

The taste of rabbit is very delicate, so you don't want to overpower it with strong or sour flavors.

Fresh, woody-stemmed herbs such as rosemary, sage and thyme are good choices. Parsley, bay leaf, basil, coriander and lemon grass go well with rabbit recipes. Allspice berries add a nice layer of flavor. If it goes well with chicken, it will do nicely with rabbit.

Marinades

Marinating your rabbit is especially important if it's an older animal. The flesh may have a gamey flavor, and you may need to marinade the meat for 24 hours in the refrigerator.

There are tons of marinade recipes available and you can certainly tailor one to fit your family's taste preferences.

Here are just a few samples of typical marinades.

Marinade with Allspice

2 cups chicken broth
1 teaspoon allspice
2 bay leaves
1 teaspoon thyme
If you like, add 2 cups red wine.

Marinade with Honey and Lemon

Olive oil
4 peeled garlic cloves
Zest and juice of one lemon
1 teaspoon honey
1 handful each fresh thyme and rosemary

Rabbit in Cream

2 small or 1 large rabbit, cut up (approx. 3 lbs. meat)
1 can sliced mushrooms, drained (4 oz.)
1 onion finely chopped
3 tablespoons cooked bacon pieces
1/2 teaspoon thyme
1 cup beef bouillon
2 tablespoons lemon juice
1 cup sour cream
3 tablespoons flour

Marinate rabbit overnight in salted water (a few tablespoons of salt) in refrigerator. Drain and pat rabbit dry. Place rabbit, mushrooms, onion, bacon and thyme in a slow cooker. Add bouillon, and stir to moisten well. Cover and cook on low for 6 to 8 hours. When rabbit is cooked, remove rabbit to a warm dish and turn slow cooker to high. Combine lemon juice, sour cream and flour. Add to the juices in crockpot and cook until juice is thickened. Serve sauce over rabbit. Yield: 6 servings.

Nutrition Facts

Serving Size 298 g

Amount Per Serving

Calories 569	Calories from Fat 250
	% Daily Value*
Total Fat 27.8g	**43%**
Saturated Fat 11.0g	**55%**
Trans Fat 0.0g	
Cholesterol 206mg	**69%**
Sodium 465mg	**19%**
Total Carbohydrates 5.7g	**2%**
Protein 69.2g	

Vitamin A 5%	•	Vitamin C 5%
Calcium 9%	•	Iron 32%

Nutrition Grade B-
* Based on a 2000 calorie diet

Hasenpfeffer (Rabbit Stew)

2 lb. rabbit
1 quart vinegar
2 tablespoons salt
1 tablespoon peppercorns
1 tablespoon pickling spice
2 large onions, sliced
1 cup cold water
2 tablespoons flour
2 tablespoons vegetable oil
1 teaspoon cinnamon
1/2 teaspoon allspice

Cut the rabbit into serving portions. Combine vinegar, salt, peppercorns, pickling spice and 1 onion. Pour over rabbit and marinate in refrigerator overnight, stirring occasionally. Drain, cover with water and bring to a boil. Simmer for 1 1/2 hours until tender. Remove meat and strain broth. Mix the cup of cold water with 2 tablespoons flour. Heat vegetable oil in a large skillet, blend in mixed water and flour, stirring constantly. Cook until thickened. Add rabbit, strained broth, allspice, cinnamon and remaining onion and simmer for 1 hour. Yield: 4 servings.

Nutrition Facts

Serving Size 623 g

Amount Per Serving

Calories 608	Calories from Fat 227
	% Daily Value*
Total Fat 25.3g	39%
Saturated Fat 6.8g	34%
Trans Fat 0.0g	
Cholesterol 186mg	62%
Sodium 3613mg	151%
Total Carbohydrates 13.9g	5%
Dietary Fiber 2.2g	9%
Sugars 4.2g	
Protein 67.4g	
Vitamin A 0%	Vitamin C 10%
Calcium 10%	Iron 36%

Nutrition Grade B
* Based on a 2000 calorie diet

Rabbit Pie

1/4 cup margarine
1/4 cup onion, chopped
1/2 cup green pepper, chopped
1/4 cup flour
2 1/2 cups rabbit broth (or water with 4 chicken bouillon cubes)
1/8 teaspoon salt
1/8 teaspoon pepper
1/2 teaspoon Accent
3 1/2 cups cooked rabbit meat, coarsely cut
1 unbaked pie crust

Heat margarine in a large skillet. Add green pepper and onion. Cook for 5 minutes over low heat. Mix in flour and cook until boiling. Add the broth gradually, stirring constantly. Cook until thick and smooth, stirring frequently. Add salt and pepper, and accent. Add rabbit meat to the sauce and heat through.

Pour mixture into a shallow baking dish or pan, place pastry over casserole and cut slits for steam to escape. Fit to top of dish or pan, crimping the edges of the crust. Bake the pie in hot oven 425 degrees for 15 to 20 minutes, or until crust browns and sauce bubbles. Yield: Serves 4.

Nutrition Facts

Serving Size 435 g

Amount Per Serving

Calories 612 — Calories from Fat 326

% Daily Value*

Total Fat 36.2g	56%
Saturated Fat 5.6g	28%
Cholesterol 0mg	0%
Sodium 533mg	22%
Total Carbohydrates 23.3g	8%
Dietary Fiber 2.0g	8%
Sugars 0.7g	
Protein 44.9g	

Vitamin A 11% • Vitamin C 16%
Calcium 2% • Iron 8%

Nutrition Grade C-
* Based on a 2000 calorie diet

Rabbit in Mustard Sauce

2 small rabbits, disjointed, cut into pieces (approx. 3 lbs.)
1/2 cup flour
1/8 teaspoon salt
1/8 teaspoon pepper
1/8 teaspoon nutmeg
1/2 cup margarine
1 tablespoon oil
4 slices lean bacon, chopped fine
6 green onions (tops removed), chopped fine
1 clove garlic, minced
1 tablespoon fresh parsley, chopped
1 bay leaf, crumbled
1/4 teaspoon thyme
1/2 cup white wine
1/2 cup water
2 egg yolks, slightly beaten
2 tablespoons prepared mustard
1/2 pint heavy cream

Pat the rabbit pieces dry. Dust each piece with flour and sprinkle with salt, pepper and nutmeg. Melt margarine and oil in a Dutch oven or large, heavy skillet and add bacon. Brown rabbit pieces over medium heat. Then add onions, garlic, parsley, bay leaf and thyme. Pour the wine and water over all. Cover and simmer until rabbit pieces are tender, about 45 minutes to an hour. Transfer rabbit to heated serving dish and keep warm.

Skim excess fat from pot and strain remaining juices into saucepan. Stir the egg yolks and mustard into the cream. Add to the strained sauce and cook, stirring, over low heat until heated through. Pour over rabbit pieces. Yield: Serves 6.

Nutrition Facts

Serving Size 384 g

Amount Per Serving

Calories 925   Calories from Fat 542

	% Daily Value*
Total Fat 60.3g	**93%**
Saturated Fat 20.6g	**103%**
Trans Fat 0.0g	
Cholesterol 332mg	**111%**
Sodium 855mg	**36%**
Total Carbohydrates 12.0g	**4%**
Dietary Fiber 0.9g	**4%**
Sugars 0.7g	
Protein 76.5g	

Vitamin A 31%	•	Vitamin C 7%
Calcium 11%	•	Iron 37%

Nutrition Grade C-

* Based on a 2000 calorie diet

Rabbit Fricasse

2 rabbits (approx. 3 lbs.)
1 onion, chopped
1/2 teaspoon pepper
1/8 teaspoon of nutmeg
1/8 teaspoon of mace
2 cups rabbit stock
2 eggs, beaten
1 tablespoon butter
1 cup milk
2 tablespoons flour
Juice of 1 lemon

Clean and wash rabbits in cold water. Cut and soak in salted water for at least 1 hour (a few tablespoons of salt). Drain, put rabbits in saucepan and cover with fresh water. Add onion, pepper, nutmeg and mace. Cover and simmer 1 hour. Remove meat and place meat in oven to keep warm. Measure out 2 cups of the rabbit stock. Add beaten eggs and butter to the stock. Thicken with flour mixed with milk. Bring to a boil and remove from heat. Add lemon juice, stirring constantly and pour over meat. Yield: Serves 6.

Nutrition Facts

Serving Size 401 g

Amount Per Serving

Calories 523	Calories from Fat 203
	% Daily Value*
Total Fat 22.5g	35%
Saturated Fat 7.7g	38%
Trans Fat 0.0g	
Cholesterol 249mg	83%
Sodium 161mg	7%
Total Carbohydrates 5.9g	2%
Sugars 3.0g	
Protein 69.6g	

Vitamin A 3%	•	Vitamin C 3%
Calcium 6%	•	Iron 31%

Nutrition Grade B
* Based on a 2000 calorie diet

Rabbit Casserole

6 slices bacon, cut in squares
1 rabbit, cut in serving portions *(approx. 2 lbs.)*
1/4 cup flour
1 teaspoon salt
1/4 teaspoon pepper
1/4 teaspoon marjoram
1/2 teaspoon Accent® seasoning
4 medium potatoes, thinly sliced
2 small onions, sliced
2 1/2 cups hot water
2 bouillon cubes

Fry bacon slowly until lightly browned. Remove from pan and pour off half the fat. Mix the flour, salt and pepper, marjoram and Accent. Reserve 2 tablespoons of the flour mixture. Dip the rabbit pieces in the remaining flour mixture. Brown in the bacon fat.

Transfer rabbit to a casserole dish. Cover rabbit meat with potato and onion slices. Sprinkle with reserved flour mixture. Dissolve bouillon cubes in hot water. Add hot bouillon water to the casserole dish. Cover and cook at 350 degrees F for 2 hours. Remove cover for last 15 minutes to brown. Serve with bacon squares on top. Yield: Serves 4.

Nutrition Facts

Serving Size 692 g

Amount Per Serving

Calories 949	Calories from Fat 383

	% Daily Value*
Total Fat 42.6g	**65%**
Saturated Fat 13.4g	**67%**
Trans Fat 0.0g	
Cholesterol 249mg	**83%**
Sodium 2392mg	**100%**
Total Carbohydrates 44.0g	**15%**
Dietary Fiber 6.0g	**24%**
Sugars 4.2g	
Protein 92.1g	

Vitamin A 1%	•	Vitamin C 74%
Calcium 9%	•	Iron 42%

Nutrition Grade B
* Based on a 2000 calorie diet

Baked Rabbit

2 small rabbits, cut into pieces (approx. 3 lbs.)
2 eggs, lightly beaten
1 cup dry bread crumbs
2 tablespoons margarine
2 tablespoons canola oil
2 cups chicken broth
2 cloves
2 medium onions

Dip rabbit pieces in egg, then coat with bread crumbs. Heat margarine and oil in large skillet and brown the meat on all sides. Transfer skillet contents to shallow roasting pan and pour in enough chicken broth to nearly cover meat. Stick a clove into each onion. Add onions and bake at 350 degrees F for about an hour or until meat is tender. Yield: Serves 6.

Nutrition Facts

Serving Size 386 g

Amount Per Serving

Calories 641	Calories from Fat 267
	% Daily Value*
Total Fat 29.6g	46%
Saturated Fat 7.2g	36%
Trans Fat 0.0g	
Cholesterol 241mg	80%
Sodium 559mg	23%
Total Carbohydrates 16.8g	6%
Dietary Fiber 1.4g	6%
Sugars 3.0g	
Protein 72.2g	
Vitamin A 5% •	Vitamin C 5%
Calcium 10% •	Iron 36%

Nutrition Grade B
* Based on a 2000 calorie diet

Barbecue Baked Rabbit

1 fryer rabbit, cut into serving portions (approx. 2 lbs.)
1 cup vegetable oil
2/3 cup vinegar
3 tablespoons sugar
3 tablespoons ketchup
1 tablespoon grated onion
1 1/2 teaspoons salt
1 tablespoon mustard
1 tablespoon Worcestershire sauce
1 clove garlic
Dash of hot pepper seasoning

Combine all ingredients, except rabbit in bowl and mix. Place rabbit in 13x10 inch pan; pour sauce over rabbit. Cover with foil and bake in oven at 350 degrees for 1/2 hour. Remove the foil, turn the rabbit pieces and spoon sauce on the pieces. Cook uncovered for an additional 1/2 hour, basting occasionally. Yield: 4 servings.

Nutrition Facts

Serving Size 354 g

Amount Per Serving

Calories 1,005	Calories from Fat 664

	% Daily Value*
Total Fat 73.8g	113%
Saturated Fat 16.2g	81%
Trans Fat 0.0g	
Cholesterol 186mg	62%
Sodium 1148mg	48%
Total Carbohydrates 14.9g	5%
Dietary Fiber 0.5g	2%
Sugars 13.2g	
Protein 66.9g	

Vitamin A 2%	•	Vitamin C 4%
Calcium 7%	•	Iron 31%

Nutrition Grade C
* Based on a 2000 calorie diet

SQUIRREL RECIPES

Squirrel

Tips for Cooking Squirrel

Squirrels are found in many parts of the United States, and the largest species is the fox squirrel. The fox squirrel ranges through the eastern United States and southern Canada and has been introduced into California. It is found as far west as the Dakotas, Colorado and Texas. It can weigh as much as 2.2 pounds.

The Eastern Grey Squirrel shares much of the same territory as the Fox Squirrel, although it is found as far south as Florida. It weighs between 14 ounces and 1.3 pounds.

The Western Grey Squirrel is found along the Pacific coast from California to Canada. Its weight varies from 14 ounces to just over 2 pounds.

Squirrels are scavengers, and if they don't have access to their preferred diet, they'll eat whatever they can find. If you're hunting squirrel in hardwood forests where there are ample nuts and acorns, you'll bring home meat that's very tasty.

Squirrels that have to forage for human scraps and garbage will have a very different flavor. You are what you eat can certainly be applied in this case.

A three ounce serving of squirrel meat has only 147 calories and four grams of fat. It's a good source of iron and has no carbohydrates. It also is a good source of B6, B12 and niacin. Since it has very little fat content, the meat can be dry and will become tough if overcooked.

General Cooking Tips

The meatiest parts of a squirrel are the hind legs and the backstraps. Soak squirrel meat in a mixture of vinegar, water and salt for two hours before cooking.

Parboil squirrel before grilling to tenderize the meat.

Young squirrel is more tender than their elderly relatives and do not need to be tenderized.

Chicken recipes are all good choices for preparing squirrel meat. The meat is less fatty and a bit firmer, so you will need to add oil or grease to your recipe to compensate for this.

Squirrels have scent glands in the upper back of their thighs. These should be removed without puncturing them.

Be careful when handling and skinning a squirrel. Before skinning, dunk the squirrel in a bucket of water or thoroughly wet the fur with a hose to prevent the hair from getting to the meat. The hair will not rinse off and must be picked away piece by piece. Guests do not appreciate picking bits of hair from between their teeth while dining.

Southern Fried Squirrel

2 squirrels
1 onion, chopped
1 carrot, chopped
1 sprig parsley, chopped
1 stalk celery, chopped
1/2 cup flour
1/2 cup corn meal
1 teaspoon baking powder
1 egg, beaten
3/4 cup milk
1 cup vegetable oil

Disjoint squirrels and drop into enough boiling water to cover squirrels. Add the onion, carrot, parsley and celery; simmer until squirrel is tender, about 45 minutes. Dry squirrel with paper towels. Mix the flour, corn meal and baking powder together. Mix the egg and milk together, add to the flour mixture. Dip squirrel pieces into the batter and drop into hot oil. Deep-fry until golden brown. Yield: Serves 4.

Nutrition Facts

Serving Size 243 g

Amount Per Serving

Calories 656	Calories from Fat 515
	% Daily Value*
Total Fat 57.2g	88%
Saturated Fat 11.6g	58%
Trans Fat 0.0g	
Cholesterol 45mg	15%
Sodium 51mg	2%
Total Carbohydrates 32.4g	11%
Dietary Fiber 2.9g	12%
Sugars 4.4g	
Protein 6.5g	

Vitamin A 55%	•	Vitamin C 6%
Calcium 8%	•	Iron 10%

Nutrition Grade C+
* Based on a 2000 calorie diet

Squirrel Fricassee

1 large squirrel, disjointed, cut into pieces
3 tablespoons baking soda
1/2 cup flour
1/2 teaspoon salt
1/4 teaspoon pepper
3 slices bacon, chopped fine
1 onion, chopped fine
2 teaspoons lemon juice
1 large apple, cored and diced
1 1/2 cups chicken stock
1 cup milk
1/4 cup flour

Soak the squirrel overnight in salt water (about 2 tablespoons of salt). Rinse and pat dry. Mix together flour, salt and pepper. Roll meat in mixture and coat evenly. In a large, heavy skillet, slowly fry the bacon. Remove bacon and set aside. Turn up heat and brown the squirrel meat in the bacon fat. Sprinkle with onion and lemon juice. Return bacon to pan and add apple and chicken stock and bring to a boil.

Place squirrel in a slow cooker, cover the meat with the broth and cook on low for 6 hours or until the meat is very tender.

Remove squirrel and apples to a plate and keep hot. Pour some of the liquid from the slow cooker into a saucepan, mix milk and flour together and add to liquid. Bring to a boil, stirring constantly. Add more flour and milk mixture if it needs thickening. Serve over squirrel. Yield: Serves 3.

NUTRITION FACTS PER SERVING: (SALT WATER THE SQUIRREL WAS SOAKED IN IS NOT INCLUDED IN NUTRITION FACTS BELOW.)

Nutrition Facts

Serving Size 416 g

Amount Per Serving

Calories 317	Calories from Fat 92

% Daily Value*

Total Fat 10.2g	**16%**
Saturated Fat 3.8g	**19%**
Trans Fat 0.0g	
Cholesterol 28mg	**9%**
Sodium 5021mg	**209%**
Total Carbohydrates 42.2g	**14%**
Dietary Fiber 3.3g	**13%**
Sugars 13.9g	
Protein 13.8g	

Vitamin A 1%	Vitamin C 13%
Calcium 4%	Iron 11%

Nutrition Grade B

* Based on a 2000 calorie diet

Squirrel Stew

2 squirrels
10 cups water
3 medium potatoes, cubed
2 onions, chopped
3 to 4 carrots, thinly sliced
2 teaspoons salt
1 teaspoon pepper
2 cups canned tomatoes with juice

Clean, wash and cut squirrel into serving size pieces. Put in pot, add cold water and bring to a boil. Add potatoes, onions, carrots, salt and pepper. Bring back to a boil, reduce heat. Cover and simmer until meat falls from bones, 1 1/2 to 2 hours. Add tomatoes with juice and simmer 1 more hour. Yield: Serves 4.

Nutrition Facts

Serving Size 981 g

Amount Per Serving

Calories 166	Calories from Fat 5

	% Daily Value*
Total Fat 0.5g	1%
Trans Fat 0.0g	
Cholesterol 0mg	0%
Sodium 1228mg	51%
Total Carbohydrates 37.9g	13%
Dietary Fiber 7.1g	28%
Sugars 8.3g	
Protein 4.4g	

Vitamin A 166%	Vitamin C 80%
Calcium 7%	Iron 8%

Nutrition Grade A
* Based on a 2000 calorie diet

GAME AND FOWL MARINADES

Marinades

Venison, Geese or Duck Marinade

1/2 cup soy sauce
1/2 cup vegetable oil
1/2 cup sherry or sake
1/3 cup lemon or pineapple juice
2 cloves, crushed
2 tablespoons sugar
1 teaspoon ginger
1 teaspoon salt

Combine all the ingredients and mix well. If grilling, reserve part of the marinade for basting. Marinate several hours or overnight in the refrigerator.

Best Venison Marinade

1 teaspoon ginger
1 teaspoon dry mustard
1 teaspoon Accent® seasoning
1/2 cup soy sauce
1/4 cup vegetable oil
3 cloves garlic, chopped, or 3 teaspoons garlic powder
1 tablespoon molasses

Mix all ingredients together. Marinate venison several hours or overnight in the refrigerator.

Soy-Onion Basting Sauce

1 teaspoon cornstarch
1 tablespoon brown sugar
2 tablespoons soy sauce
2 tablespoons lemon juice
2 tablespoons water
2 tablespoons green onion with tops, chopped
1 tablespoon margarine
1 clove garlic, minced

In saucepan, blend cornstarch and brown sugar. Add soy sauce, lemon juice, water, onion, margarine and garlic. Cook and stir till thick and bubbly. Use to baste fish or poultry during last 20 minutes of barbecuing. Can also marinate overnight, then baste with the marinade while grilling.

Basic Seasoning Salt

26 oz. table salt
4 tablespoons white sugar
1 tablespoon garlic salt
1 tablespoon onion salt
2 tablespoons paprika
2 tablespoons dill salt
2 tablespoons celery salt
4 tablespoons black pepper
2 tablespoons white pepper

Mix all ingredients together thoroughly; store in covered jar in dry place. Let stand several days before use. For spicier seasoning, add 1 tablespoon mace and/or nutmeg. For hotter seasoning, add 1 tablespoon curry powder and/or dry mustard. Good with wild game (season while cooking) and fish.

FISH RECIPES

Fish

Tips for Cooking Fish

Fish is a great source of protein for health conscious cooks. Most types of fish are low in fat, cholesterol and are good sources of B vitamins. Oily fish also are rich in vitamin A and D. A number of fish also provide significant calcium. Eating oil-rich fish such as trout and salmon provides Omega-3 fatty acid. This essential nutrient can reduce the risk of heart attack, reduces blood pressure and is thought to reduce the painful inflammation that plagues rheumatoid arthritis suffers.

Along with all these other benefits, fish is low in calories. It's a great source of protein for a low fat diet and weight watchers in general. One serving of fish provides over 30 percent of the recommended dietary needs for a typical adult, and it can be prepared in almost limitless ways.

Fish can be baked, steamed, grilled, broiled, fried or cooked in a slow cooker. Since overcooking can result in dry, tasteless fish, be careful of your cooking time. A general rule is that fish should be cooked 10 minutes for each inch of thickness. However, this rule does not apply to microwaving or deep-frying. Fish should be cooked to an internal temperature of 145 degrees Fahrenheit.

Fish Cooking Times

You should carefully monitor cooking time and temperature for your fish. Since it cooks quickly and is easily overcooked, it's not something you can toss in a pan and leave unattended. The following information applies to baked, grilled, steamed, fried and deep-fried fish.

Baked Fish

Baked fish should be cooked at 350 degrees Fahrenheit. Whether it's a whole fish, fillets or steaks, a three to five pound piece of fish should cook for 25 to 30 minutes.

Pan Fried Fish

Pan fried fish should be cooked over a medium heat to avoid scorching and burning. Fried fish should be turned once for thorough cooking. Whole fish should cook between 8 and 15 minutes, depending upon the thickness. Fillets that are 3/4" thick should fry for 7 to 9 minutes, and 1" thick fish steaks will require 9 to 10 minutes of cooking.

Deep Fried Fish

With oil set at 350 degrees, cook whole fish and 3/4" thick fillets for three to five minutes. Thick, 1" steaks may require four to six minutes to cook properly.

Grilled Fish

Using a moderate heat, place your grill four inches from the heat source. You will turn the fish once during the grilling process to cook the meat through. Depending on size, whole fish will require 10 to 20 minutes of cooking time. Fillets that are 3/4" thick will cook in 7 to 9 minutes, and 1" steaks will be done in 9 to 10 minutes.

Steamed Fish

Using a steamer and gently boiling water, whole fish and 3/4" fillets will be ready to serve in 10 to 12 minutes. Steaks that are 1" thick may take from 10 to 15 minutes to cook completely.

Please note that all the cooking times are estimates. The type and thickness of fish, as well as the reliability of your heat source, may require time and heat adjustments to produce flaky and flavorful fish.

When in doubt, use the fork test. Gently separate the fish with a fork. If the meat is opaque and comes apart with a flaky texture, it's done. Don't hesitate, as overcooked fish is tough, dry and flavorless.

Fish Categories

Based on the texture of the flesh, fish fall into three categories. These categories are soft-textured, flaky-textured and firm-textured fish. Many cooking methods overlap for some or all the categories of fish, but there are some general recommendations for each type of fish.

Soft-Textured Fish

These fish have delicate flesh, so they must be handled carefully. Mild flavored varieties of this fish include sea trout, sole and flounder. Stronger flavored fish like herring and bluefish are also in this category. These fish are best when baked, steamed, microwaved or sautéed.

Flaky-Textured Fish

This category includes fish whose flesh separates into large flakes when cooked. Trout, perch, whitefish and mullet fall into the mild-flavored fish in this category, while salmon, mackerel, smelt and sardines encompass the strong flavored fish that are flaky in texture. Cooking methods include baking, broiling, grilling, microwaving, poaching, sautéing and steaming.

Firm-Textured Fish

Some firm-textured fish has flesh that resembles beef or chicken. Mild-flavored varieties include catfish, carp, striped bass and mahi-mahi. Strong-flavored fish are tuna and monkfish. This hearty meat can stand up to stir-frying and grilling very well. It is also often baked, broiled, steamed or microwaved.

Cooking Tips for Fish

Wrangling large, whole fish in and out of a baking pan can be rather traumatic. To keep your blood pressure down and your fingers scorch-free, make a sturdy bed of aluminum foil for your fish. Grease the foil and make sure it's wide enough to use as a sling when placing and removing the meat. You'll also minimize your cleanup time.

If you plan to batter fry your fish, make sure the batter is cold. Cold batter and hot oil will prevent the batter from absorbing much oil. Use a thermometer to make sure your oil heats up to the proper temperature if you are cooking batches of fish.

While you're cooking those batches of fish, line a tray with paper towels and fit the tray with a wire rack. Place the cooked batches of fish on the rack and keep in a warm oven until it's time to serve your hungry crew.

If you're broiling or grilling lean fish like bass or walleye, basting occasionally adds flavor and keeps the flesh from drying out.

When baking a whole fish, leave the head and tail intact. This results in a moister, more flavorful fish. Just discreetly remove the offending portions before serving if you have delicate diners at your table.

If you're broiling fish fillets, tuck the thin tail end underneath for even cooking.

A simple, foolproof utensil for grilling fish and other delicate foods is a grilling basket. These handy devices mean no more broken pieces of fish falling into the embers or gas flames. Just remember to oil the basket before adding your fish to prevent sticking.

Citrus-Marinated Fish Fillets

1 pound fresh or frozen fish fillets
2/3 cup lime juice
2 tablespoons vegetable oil
4 teaspoons honey
2/3 cup water
1 teaspoon dried dill weed
1/2 teaspoon salt

Thaw fish, if frozen. Separate fillets or cut into 4 serving-sized portions. Put fish in a shallow pan. For marinade, mix lime juice, vegetable oil, honey, water, dill weed and salt. Divide marinade into 2 equal portions, reserve and store one portion in refrigerator. Pour the other portion of marinade over the fish. Cover and refrigerate for 3 hours or overnight, turning fish occasionally.

Remove fish from the pan, disposing of used marinade. Place fish on slightly greased rack of a broiler pan. Broil fish 4 inches from heat until fish flakes easily when tested with fork. (Allow 5 minutes for each 1/2" thickness.) Baste fish often with reserved portion of marinade during broiling. Yield: 2 servings.

Nutrition Facts
Serving Size 417 g

Amount Per Serving

Calories 371	Calories from Fat 141

	% Daily Value*
Total Fat 15.7g	**24%**
Saturated Fat 3.6g	**18%**
Trans Fat 0.0g	
Cholesterol 110mg	**37%**
Sodium 667mg	**28%**
Total Carbohydrates 18.7g	**6%**
Sugars 12.9g	
Protein 42.7g	

Vitamin A 1%	•	Vitamin C 42%
Calcium 6%	•	Iron 15%

Nutrition Grade D+
* Based on a 2000 calorie diet

Baked Whole Fish with Mushrooms

3 1/2 lbs. whole striped bass or rainbow trout
1/2 cup flour
1/8 teaspoon salt
1/8 teaspoon pepper
3 tablespoons olive oil
2 tablespoons butter
1 rib celery, thinly sliced
1 medium carrot, thinly sliced
1 can mushrooms, thinly sliced (8 oz.)
1/4 cup parsley, minced
2 tablespoons of dry white wine
1/4 teaspoon salt
1/4 teaspoon pepper
1 1/3 cups spaghetti sauce with mushrooms
1/4 cup green onions, sliced
Lemon wedges for garnish

Coat fish with flour; sprinkle with 1/8 teaspoon salt and pepper. Sauté in oil and butter in large skillet until brown, remove. Sauté celery, carrots, mushrooms, parsley, wine, 1/4 teaspoon salt and pepper for 5 minutes. Spread 2/3 of the celery mixture on oven-proof platter; spoon 2/3 cup sauce over it. Stuff fish with remaining celery mixture; arrange on platter. Spoon remaining sauce on fish. Bake at 425 degrees until fish is tender, about 20 minutes. Sprinkle with green onions; garnish with lemon. Yield: 6 servings.

Nutrition Facts

Serving Size 403 g

Amount Per Serving

Calories 686 — Calories from Fat 306

	% Daily Value*
Total Fat 34.0g	**52%**
Saturated Fat 7.4g	**37%**
Trans Fat 0.0g	
Cholesterol 206mg	**69%**
Sodium 802mg	**33%**
Total Carbohydrates 17.8g	**6%**
Dietary Fiber 2.6g	**10%**
Sugars 5.9g	
Protein 73.4g	

Vitamin A 49%	•	Vitamin C 17%
Calcium 17%	•	Iron 37%

Nutrition Grade B-

* Based on a 2000 calorie diet

Southern Bass Chowder

1/4 cup butter
1 tablespoon flour
1/2 cup scallions, chopped
1 garlic clove, minced
1/4 cup green pepper, chopped
1/2 cup celery, chopped
1/2 cup zucchini, chopped
1 can tomatoes (16 oz.)
1/2 cup dry sherry
1 tablespoon lemon juice
3 drops Tabasco® sauce
1/8 teaspoon salt
1/8 teaspoon pepper
1/2 tablespoon thyme
2 lbs. bass fillets

Melt butter in skillet. Blend in flour and stir over heat for 2 minutes. Add scallions, garlic, green pepper, celery and zucchini, and cook until vegetables are soft. Chop tomatoes into small pieces and add to skillet. Combine all other ingredients except fish, and mix well. Simmer uncovered for 1 1/2 hours, adding a little water if necessary, stirring occasionally. Place fish fillets on top of sauce. Cover and increase heat. Cook for 10 minutes or until fish flakes apart easily with a fork. Serve over rice or grits. Yield: 4 servings.

NUTRITION FACTS PER SERVING: (RICE OR GRITS NOT INCLUDED)

Nutrition Facts

Serving Size 409 g

Amount Per Serving

Calories 427	Calories from Fat 166
	% Daily Value*
Total Fat 18.5g	**28%**
Saturated Fat 8.8g	**44%**
Cholesterol 264mg	**88%**
Sodium 613mg	**26%**
Total Carbohydrates 10.0g	**3%**
Dietary Fiber 3.0g	**12%**
Sugars 4.9g	
Protein 53.6g	

Vitamin A 27%	•	Vitamin C 35%
Calcium 9%	•	Iron 20%

Nutrition Grade B

* Based on a 2000 calorie diet

Seasoned Fish

1/2 pkg. oyster crackers, crushed (6 oz. pkg.)
1/2 teaspoon lemon pepper
1/2 teaspoon seasoned salt
1/2 cup vegetable oil
1 teaspoon dill weed
1 envelope Hidden Valley® salad dressing (1 oz.)
9 fish fillets

Mix together crackers, lemon pepper, salt, oil, dill weed and salad dressing. Preheat oven to 375 degrees F. Pour 1/2 cup oil onto a cookie sheet with sides, until bottom is covered. Put cookie sheet in oven while coating fish. Coat fish fillets with cracker mixture. Put fillets on cookie sheet when oil is hot and return to oven. Turn fillets several times until golden brown, or fry 6 1/2 minutes on each side. Yield: 9 servings.

Nutrition Facts

Serving Size 116 g

Amount Per Serving

Calories 366	Calories from Fat 218
	% Daily Value*
Total Fat 24.2g	37%
Saturated Fat 4.5g	22%
Trans Fat 0.0g	
Cholesterol 31mg	10%
Sodium 883mg	37%
Total Carbohydrates 24.4g	8%
Dietary Fiber 0.5g	2%
Protein 14.0g	

Vitamin A 1%	•	Vitamin C 0%
Calcium 2%	•	Iron 14%

Nutrition Grade C
* Based on a 2000 calorie diet

Lemon Fish Roll-Ups

1/3 cup butter
2 teaspoons salt
1/4 teaspoon pepper
1/3 cup lemon juice
1 1/3 cups cooked white rice
1 cup sharp cheddar cheese, shredded
1 package frozen broccoli, thawed, chopped (10 oz.)
8 fish fillets
Paprika

In small saucepan, melt butter. Add salt, pepper and lemon juice. Set aside. In medium bowl, combine rice, cheese, broccoli and 1/4 cup of the lemon mixture. Place 1/8th of the rice mixture on top of each of the 8 fish fillets and roll the fillets up. Place seam-side down in 11x7-inch baking dish. Top with remaining sauce, then sprinkle with paprika. Bake at 375 degrees F for 25 minutes or until fish flakes with fork. Yield: 8 servings.

Nutrition Facts

Serving Size 169 g

Amount Per Serving

Calories 377	Calories from Fat 213
	% Daily Value*
Total Fat 23.7g	36%
Saturated Fat 10.5g	53%
Cholesterol 66mg	22%
Sodium 1302mg	54%
Total Carbohydrates 23.9g	8%
Dietary Fiber 1.7g	7%
Sugars 0.8g	
Protein 18.7g	
Vitamin A 15%	Vitamin C 32%
Calcium 14%	Iron 14%

Nutrition Grade B-
* Based on a 2000 calorie diet

Baked Stuffed Fish

2 to 3 lbs. fish
1/2 teaspoon salt
1/8 teaspoon pepper
5 slices dried bread, crusts removed
1 large onion, chopped
2 oz. butter
1/4 teaspoon parsley or sage
2 egg yolks, beaten
3 strips bacon
1 tablespoon butter
1/2 cup hot water
Nonstick cooking spray

Clean and scale fish, removing head and tail if desired. Rub with salt and pepper inside and out.

To make stuffing, soak bread in water and squeeze dry. Tear bread into pieces. Sauté onion in butter. Add bread pieces and parsley or sage. Remove from heat and add beaten egg yolks. Stuff fish. Close opening with toothpicks. Place in a baking dish sprayed lightly with cooking spray. Lay strips of bacon over fish. Bake fish in 425 degree F oven. Allow 15 minutes per pound up to 4 pounds, and 5 minutes for each additional pound. Baste fish every 10 minutes with butter mixed with 1/2 cup hot water. Fish is done when it flakes easily with fork. Yield: 4 servings.

Nutrition Facts

Serving Size 460 g

Amount Per Serving

Calories 557	Calories from Fat 236

% Daily Value*

Total Fat 26.2g	**40%**
Saturated Fat 13.4g	**67%**
Trans Fat 0.0g	
Cholesterol 324mg	**108%**
Sodium 926mg	**39%**
Total Carbohydrates 9.8g	**3%**
Dietary Fiber 0.9g	**4%**
Sugars 2.1g	
Protein 71.3g	

Vitamin A 12% •	Vitamin C 5%
Calcium 10% •	Iron 24%

Nutrition Grade D+

* Based on a 2000 calorie diet

Fish in Creole Sauce

2 tablespoons margarine
1/4 cup onion, chopped
1 clove garlic, minced
6 green olives, minced
2 cups stewed tomatoes
1/2 green pepper, chopped
1/2 bay leaf
3 beef bouillon cubes
1/8 teaspoon thyme
2 teaspoons parsley, chopped
1 teaspoon sugar
1/3 teaspoon salt
Cayenne pepper to taste
1/4 cup white wine
1/4 cup mushrooms, sliced
5 Northern pike fillets, boned and cut in 2" chunks
25 frozen medium shrimp
6 cups cooked rice

Melt margarine and sauté onion, garlic and olives about 2 minutes. Add and cook the rest of the ingredients, except the fillets and shrimp, until sauce is thickened, about 50 minutes. Add fillet chunks and 20 to 25 frozen shrimp to the sauce and cook for 15 minutes or until fish is cooked through. Serve over hot rice. Yield: 6 servings.

Nutrition Facts

Serving Size 710 g

Amount Per Serving	
Calories 981	Calories from Fat 226
	% Daily Value*
Total Fat 25.2g	**39%**
Saturated Fat 4.6g	**23%**
Trans Fat 0.0g	
Cholesterol 749mg	**250%**
Sodium 1622mg	**68%**
Total Carbohydrates 67.1g	**22%**
Dietary Fiber 2.6g	**10%**
Sugars 3.8g	
Protein 113.8g	
Vitamin A 14% •	Vitamin C 26%
Calcium 28% •	Iron 60%
Nutrition Grade D	
* Based on a 2000 calorie diet	

Company Fillets

2 cups onions, sliced
White fish, cut in 8 pieces (32 oz.)
3/4 cup mayonnaise
1/4 cup parmesan cheese
2 teaspoons lemon juice
1 teaspoon Worcestershire sauce
1/2 teaspoon paprika
2 teaspoons dried parsley
Nonstick cooking spray

Preheat oven to 350 degrees F. Spray a large skillet with cooking spray and sauté onion for 10 minutes or until tender. Spray a 9 x 13 inch baking dish with cooking spray and evenly arrange fish in dish. In a bowl, combine mayonnaise, Parmesan cheese, juice, Worcestershire sauce and paprika. Spread on fillets, spoon onions on top. Bake for 25 to 30 minutes or until fish flakes easily. Just before serving, sprinkle with parsley. Yield: 8 servings.

Nutrition Facts

Serving Size 170 g

Amount Per Serving

Calories 195   Calories from Fat 76

	% Daily Value*
Total Fat 8.4g	13%
Saturated Fat 1.7g	8%
Trans Fat 0.0g	
Cholesterol 8mg	3%
Sodium 213mg	9%
Total Carbohydrates 8.3g	3%
Dietary Fiber 0.6g	2%
Sugars 2.8g	
Protein 19.9g	

Vitamin A 3%   •   Vitamin C 5%
Calcium 5%   •   Iron 1%

Nutrition Grade C-
* Based on a 2000 calorie diet

Baked Fillets of Northern Pike

1 1/2 cups of dry white wine
2 tablespoons butter
2 tablespoons onion, grated
1 bay leaf
1 cup fresh mushrooms, sliced
2 teaspoons parsley, chopped
3 tablespoons heavy cream
2 teaspoons salt
1 1/2 teaspoons white pepper
4 fillets of pike
2 tablespoons parmesan cheese
Cooking spray

Combine the wine, butter, onion, bay leaf, mushrooms and parsley in a saucepan; bring to a boil and cook over medium heat 10 minutes. Mix in the cream. Discard the bay leaf. Sprinkle the salt and pepper on the fillets. Spray cooking spray on a baking dish and arrange fillets on the dish in a single layer. Pour the sauce over the fish and sprinkle with cheese. Bake at 350 degrees F 25 to 30 minutes. Yield: 4 servings.

Nutrition Facts

Serving Size 261 g

Amount Per Serving

Calories 332	Calories from Fat 115
	% Daily Value*
Total Fat 12.8g	20%
Saturated Fat 7.1g	36%
Trans Fat 0.0g	
Cholesterol 169mg	56%
Sodium 1333mg	56%
Total Carbohydrates 4.6g	2%
Dietary Fiber 0.6g	2%
Sugars 1.3g	
Protein 32.5g	
Vitamin A 11%	Vitamin C 3%
Calcium 23%	Iron 18%

Nutrition Grade C+

* Based on a 2000 calorie diet

Easy Fish 'N' Chips

1/2 cup butter
2 potatoes, peeled and cut in 1/4" slices
3/4 cup Ritz crackers, crushed
2 tablespoons parsley
1 teaspoon paprika
3/4 teaspoon salt
1/2 teaspoon garlic powder
1 lb. frozen fish fillets, thawed

Melt butter in a 9 x 13-inch pan. Add potato slices and stir to blend. Cover with foil and bake at 350 degrees F for 20 to 25 minutes. Combine crackers, parsley, paprika, salt and garlic powder. Spoon potatoes to one side of baking dish. Dip fillets into melted butter that potatoes were in; then roll in crumb mixture. Place fillets in same baking dish with potatoes. Sprinkle with remaining crumb mixture. Return to oven and continue baking, uncovered for 20 to 30 minutes. Yield: 4 servings.

Nutrition Facts

Serving Size 255 g

Amount Per Serving

Calories 598	Calories from Fat 349
	% Daily Value*
Total Fat 38.7g	60%
Saturated Fat 19.5g	97%
Trans Fat 0.0g	
Cholesterol 112mg	37%
Sodium 1075mg	45%
Total Carbohydrates 45.3g	15%
Dietary Fiber 3.9g	16%
Sugars 2.6g	
Protein 18.9g	
Vitamin A 23%	Vitamin C 40%
Calcium 2%	Iron 9%

Nutrition Grade D+

* Based on a 2000 calorie diet

Easy Baked Fillets

4 fish fillets
1 cup shrimp, cooked and deveined
4 tablespoons mayonnaise
4 slices of lemon
Aluminum foil

Cut 4 large rectangles of aluminum foil. Put one fillet on each rectangle. Add 1/4 cup shrimp on top of each fillet and 1 tablespoon mayonnaise on top of that. Wrap foil around fish tightly and bake at 375 degrees F for 10 minutes or until fish flakes easily with fork. Serve with a slice of lemon. Yield: 4 servings.

Nutrition Facts

Serving Size 118 g

Amount Per Serving

Calories 277	Calories from Fat 146
	% Daily Value*
Total Fat 16.2g	**25%**
Saturated Fat 3.3g	**17%**
Cholesterol 46mg	**15%**
Sodium 602mg	**25%**
Total Carbohydrates 19.7g	**7%**
Dietary Fiber 0.7g	**3%**
Sugars 1.1g	
Protein 14.8g	
Vitamin A 2% •	Vitamin C 6%
Calcium 3% •	Iron 11%

Nutrition Grade C+
* Based on a 2000 calorie diet

Midwestern Fish Stew

1/4 lb. bacon, diced
1 cup onions, sliced
2 cups chicken broth
2 cups dry white wine or water
1 can stewed tomatoes (14 1/2 oz.)
1 pound new red potatoes, quartered
1 teaspoon parsley
1 teaspoon dried tarragon leaves
1 teaspoon dried thyme leaves
1/4 teaspoon pepper
1 cup red bell pepper, julienne-cut
1 cup frozen cut green beans
6 frozen mini ears of corn on the cob (or cut 3 full size ears in half)
1 1/2 lbs. boneless skinless fish, cut into 1 inch pieces

Cook bacon until almost crisp in 6-quart Dutch oven. Add onions; cook until tender. Drain. Add broth, wine, tomatoes, potatoes, parsley, tarragon, thyme and pepper. Bring to a boil. Reduce heat to low; simmer, partially covered, 20 to 25 minutes or until potatoes are almost tender. Add bell pepper, green beans, corn and fish to tomato mixture. Bring to a boil. Reduce heat to low; cover and simmer 7 to 9 minutes or until fish flakes easily with fork. Yield: 6 servings.

Nutrition Facts

Serving Size 493 g

Amount Per Serving

Calories 454	Calories from Fat 176
	% Daily Value*
Total Fat 19.6g	30%
Saturated Fat 2.8g	14%
Trans Fat 0.0g	
Cholesterol 21mg	7%
Sodium 697mg	29%
Total Carbohydrates 24.2g	8%
Dietary Fiber 3.3g	13%
Sugars 6.2g	
Protein 30.0g	
Vitamin A 13%	Vitamin C 38%
Calcium 3%	Iron 7%

Nutrition Grade C-

* Based on a 2000 calorie diet

Broiled Fish with Dijon Sauce

3 tablespoons parmesan cheese, freshly grated
2 tablespoons Dijon mustard
1/2 cup mayonnaise
1/8 teaspoon black pepper
1 lb. firm fish fillets

In a bowl, mix the cheese, mustard, mayonnaise and pepper. Spread cheese mixture on the fillets. Broil the fillets for 4 to 7 minutes, depending on the size and thickness of the fish, or just until the fish flakes with a fork. Yield: 3 servings.

Nutrition Facts

Serving Size 206 g

Amount Per Serving

Calories 532	Calories from Fat 302
	% Daily Value*
Total Fat 33.5g	**52%**
Saturated Fat 7.1g	**35%**
Trans Fat 0.0g	
Cholesterol 66mg	**22%**
Sodium 1278mg	**53%**
Total Carbohydrates 35.8g	**12%**
Dietary Fiber 1.1g	**4%**
Sugars 2.6g	
Protein 24.9g	

Vitamin A 3%	Vitamin C 0%
Calcium 9%	Iron 20%

Nutrition Grade C+
* Based on a 2000 calorie diet

Fish with Tarragon Butter

4 fish fillets

Tarragon butter:

1/4 cup butter
1/2 teaspoon tarragon, dried
1 teaspoon lemon juice
1/8 teaspoon salt
1/8 teaspoon pepper

To prepare tarragon butter:

Cream butter until fluffy and light. Blend in tarragon and lemon juice. Let stand an hour at room temperature before using.

Salt and pepper the fillets. Place on greased broiler pan and spread with tarragon butter. Broil 4" from heat until fish flakes easily with fork (about 5 minutes per half-inch thickness of fish). Serve with extra butter when the fish is served. Yield: 4 servings.

Nutrition Facts

Serving Size 107 g

Amount Per Serving

Calories 314	Calories from Fat 204
	% Daily Value*
Total Fat 22.7g	**35%**
Saturated Fat 9.9g	**49%**
Cholesterol 61mg	**20%**
Sodium 640mg	**27%**
Total Carbohydrates 15.6g	**5%**
Dietary Fiber 0.5g	**2%**
Protein 13.5g	

Vitamin A 8%	•	Vitamin C 1%
Calcium 2%	•	Iron 11%

Nutrition Grade D
* Based on a 2000 calorie diet

Fried Fish

1 1/2 lbs. fish fillets
2 eggs, separated
1 cup flour
1/4 cup milk
1/2 cup beer
1/2 teaspoon seasoned salt
1/4 teaspoon seasoned pepper
Vegetable oil for frying

Defrost fish partially; cut into 3 x 1-1/2 inch pieces. Beat egg yolks; add flour, milk, beer and seasoned salt and pepper; stir until smooth. Beat egg whites; fold in. Pat fillets dry. Dip fillets in batter, a couple pieces at a time. Fry in deep oil at 375 degrees F for 2 to 3 minutes, until golden brown and puffed. Drain on paper towels. Serve with heated vinegar, salt and ketchup. Yield: 2 to 3 servings.

Nutrition Facts

Serving Size 368 g

Amount Per Serving

Calories 828	Calories from Fat 366
	% Daily Value*
Total Fat 40.7g	63%
Saturated Fat 9.4g	47%
Cholesterol 188mg	63%
Sodium 1512mg	63%
Total Carbohydrates 73.0g	24%
Dietary Fiber 2.3g	9%
Sugars 1.4g	
Protein 42.1g	

Vitamin A 5%	Vitamin C 0%
Calcium 7%	Iron 41%

Nutrition Grade C
* Based on a 2000 calorie diet

Baked Fish Fillets

1 lb. fish fillets
2 tablespoons lemon juice
2 tablespoons butter, melted
1/4 teaspoon dill weed
1/2 teaspoon salt
1/4 teaspoon pepper
2 cups Total® cereal, crushed

Grease baking pan. If fillets are large, cut into serving sizes. Mix lemon juice and butter; reserve. Mix dill weed, salt and pepper. Dip each fillet in margarine mixture; sprinkle with salt mixture and coat with cereal. Bake, uncovered, at 350 degrees F for 20 to 30 minutes or until fish flakes easily. Yield: 4 servings.

Nutrition Facts

Serving Size 149 g

Amount Per Serving

Calories 383	Calories from Fat 181
	% Daily Value*
Total Fat 20.1g	**31%**
Saturated Fat 6.9g	**35%**
Trans Fat 0.0g	
Cholesterol 54mg	**18%**
Sodium 1030mg	**43%**
Total Carbohydrates 34.2g	**11%**
Dietary Fiber 2.6g	**11%**
Sugars 3.5g	
Protein 18.1g	
Vitamin A 11%	Vitamin C 73%
Calcium 69%	Iron 80%

Nutrition Grade A-
* Based on a 2000 calorie diet

Fillet Almondine

1/3 cup almonds, sliced or slivered
1/4 cup margarine
1 pound lean fish fillets
1/2 tablespoon salt
1 tablespoon dry white wine or lemon juice

Place almonds and margarine in a 9 inch pie plate. Microwave on high for 3 to 5 minutes until almonds are golden, stirring twice. Remove almonds with a slotted spoon; set aside. Add fillets to margarine, turning to coat. Arrange fillets in dish with thicker portions towards the outside of dish. Cover with wax paper. Microwave on high 4 to 6 minutes, until fish begins to flake when fork is inserted in thickest part. Sprinkle with salt, wine or lemon juice and reserved almonds. Yield: 4 servings.

Nutrition Facts

Serving Size 141 g

Amount Per Serving

Calories 453 — Calories from Fat 269

	% Daily Value*
Total Fat 29.9g	46%
Saturated Fat 6.8g	34%
Trans Fat 0.0g	
Cholesterol 51mg	17%
Sodium 1452mg	60%
Total Carbohydrates 28.0g	9%
Dietary Fiber 2.0g	8%
Sugars 1.4g	
Protein 18.5g	

Vitamin A 10% • Vitamin C 0%
Calcium 3% • Iron 6%

Nutrition Grade F
* Based on a 2000 calorie diet

Fish Fillets in Foil

4 fillets of fish
4 pieces aluminum foil
1 cup salsa
4 cups hot cooked white rice
Lime wedges to garnish
Nonstick cooking spray

Using a nonstick spray, spray 4 pieces of foil. Place a fish fillet on each foil. Top with 1/4 cup salsa. Fold foil, crimping edges tightly to seal. Cook on a hot barbecue grill for about 10 minutes. Remove from grill and open foil packet carefully to avoid the hot steam. Serve each fillet with the sauce on rice and garnish with lime wedges. Yield: 4 servings.

Nutrition Facts

Serving Size 220 g

Amount Per Serving

Calories 477	Calories from Fat 131
	% Daily Value*
Total Fat 14.5g	22%
Saturated Fat 4.6g	23%
Cholesterol 49mg	16%
Sodium 821mg	34%
Total Carbohydrates 66.0g	22%
Dietary Fiber 2.6g	11%
Sugars 3.1g	
Protein 20.3g	
Vitamin A 4% •	Vitamin C 2%
Calcium 3% •	Iron 17%

Nutrition Grade C
* Based on a 2000 calorie diet

Broiled Fish Fillets Au Gratin

2 pkgs. frozen broccoli (10 oz. each)
2 lbs. freshwater drum or other fish fillets
2 tablespoons butter or margarine
2 tablespoons lemon juice
1/2 cup milk
2 cups American cheese, grated

Cook broccoli until just tender. Place fish fillets in a greased, shallow baking dish. Dot with butter and sprinkle with lemon juice. Broil for about 8 minutes. Meanwhile, using a double boiler, heat cheese and milk, blend until smooth. Remove fish from broiler and arrange broccoli over fish. Pour sauce over fish and broccoli. Continue broiling on a lower shelf in broiler until golden brown. Yield: 6 servings.

Nutrition Facts

Serving Size 314 g

Amount Per Serving

Calories 600 — Calories from Fat 301

	% Daily Value*
Total Fat 33.4g	51%
Saturated Fat 14.6g	73%
Cholesterol 110mg	37%
Sodium 1354mg	56%
Total Carbohydrates 43.8g	15%
Dietary Fiber 4.2g	17%
Sugars 6.7g	
Protein 32.8g	

Vitamin A 27%	Vitamin C 67%
Calcium 25%	Iron 10%

Nutrition Grade C+
* Based on a 2000 calorie diet

Walleye Vegetarian Delight

4 walleye fillets
1/2 tablespoon lemon juice
1/2 cup white wine
1/2 tablespoon orange juice
1/8 cup butter
Vegetable stuffing (recipe below)

Place the fillets on a well-greased shallow baking pan. Drizzle with lemon and orange juice. Cover with vegetable stuffing, wine and several slices of butter. Cover with foil and bake at 350 degrees F for 20 minutes. Uncover and continue to bake for 10 to15 minutes or until fish flakes apart easily with a fork. Yield: 4 servings.

Vegetable stuffing:

1/2 cup onion, chopped
1/4 cup carrots, thinly sliced
1/2 cup celery, chopped
1/2 cup green pepper, chopped
1/4 cup butter
1 cup seasoned bread crumbs
1 cup diced tomato
1/8 teaspoon salt
1/8 teaspoon pepper

Sauté onion, carrots, celery and green pepper in butter until tender, about 10 minutes. Add the remaining ingredients and mix well.

Nutrition Facts

Serving Size 394 g

Amount Per Serving

Calories 643	Calories from Fat 325

	% Daily Value*
Total Fat 36.1g	**55%**
Saturated Fat 13.4g	**67%**
Trans Fat 0.0g	
Cholesterol 241mg	**80%**
Sodium 945mg	**39%**
Total Carbohydrates 26.1g	**9%**
Dietary Fiber 2.8g	**11%**
Sugars 4.6g	
Protein 48.2g	

Vitamin A 43%	Vitamin C 31%
Calcium 8%	Iron 10%

Nutrition Grade D-

* Based on a 2000 calorie diet

Fish Jambalaya

1 lb. freshwater drum fillets
1/2 cup bacon, chopped
1 cup onion, chopped
1 clove garlic, finely chopped
1/2 cup green pepper, chopped
1 chicken bouillon cube
1 cup boiling water
1 can tomatoes (16 oz.)
1 can tomato sauce (8 oz.)
1 cup uncooked white rice
1/4 cup parsley, chopped
1 tablespoon salt
1/4 tablespoon thyme
1/8 teaspoon ground cloves
1/8 teaspoon nutmeg
1/8 teaspoon cayenne pepper
Nonstick cooking spray

Cut fish fillets into 1-inch pieces. Fry bacon until crisp. Add onion, garlic and green pepper to bacon and sauté until onion is transparent. Dissolve chicken bouillon cube in boiling water. Add all the rest of the ingredients and pour into a 2-quart casserole dish, sprayed well with cooking spray. Cover and bake at 350 degrees F for 50 to 60 minutes or until rice is tender and fish flakes apart easily with a fork. Yield: 6 servings.

Nutrition Facts

Serving Size 299 g

Amount Per Serving

Calories 387	Calories from Fat 116
	% Daily Value*
Total Fat 12.8g	**20%**
Saturated Fat 4.1g	**21%**
Trans Fat 0.0g	
Cholesterol 41mg	**14%**
Sodium 2073mg	**86%**
Total Carbohydrates 50.7g	**17%**
Dietary Fiber 3.6g	**14%**
Sugars 6.0g	
Protein 17.3g	
Vitamin A 14%	Vitamin C 33%
Calcium 4%	Iron 16%

Nutrition Grade B-

* Based on a 2000 calorie diet

Baked Walleye with Orange Rice Stuffing

6 dressed walleye (1 to 1-1/2 lbs. each)
2 tablespoons salt
2 tablespoons vegetable oil
2 tablespoons orange juice
Orange-Rice Stuffing (recipe below)

Preheat oven to 350 degrees F. Sprinkle fish inside and out with salt and stuff with Orange-Rice Stuffing. Close openings with a toothpick and place fish into a well-greased baking pan. In a bowl, combine oil and orange juice. Brush fish with orange juice mixture and bake at 350 degrees F for 30 to 35 minutes, or until fish flakes apart easily with a fork. While baking, baste fish occasionally with orange juice mixture. When ready to serve, remove toothpicks. Yield: 8 servings.

Orange Rice Stuffing:

1 cup celery, chopped
1/4 cup onion, chopped
1/4 cup vegetable oil
3/4 cup water
1/4 cup orange juice
1 tablespoon grated orange rind
3/4 tablespoon salt
1 cup instant rice
1/2 cup toasted, slivered almonds

Sauté onions and celery in oil until tender. Add water, orange juice, orange rind and salt and bring mixture to a boil. Add rice and stir to moisten. Cover, remove from heat and set aside for 5 minutes. Add almonds.

Nutrition Facts

Serving Size 189 g

Amount Per Serving

Calories 329	Calories from Fat 133

	% Daily Value*
Total Fat 14.8g	**23%**
Saturated Fat 2.6g	**13%**
Trans Fat 0.0g	
Cholesterol 102mg	**34%**
Sodium 1602mg	**67%**
Total Carbohydrates 22.0g	**7%**
Dietary Fiber 1.4g	**6%**
Sugars 1.7g	
Protein 26.0g	

Vitamin A 3%	•	Vitamin C 13%
Calcium 16%	•	Iron 16%

Nutrition Grade B+

* Based on a 2000 calorie diet

Fish-Stuffed Green Peppers

2 large green peppers
2 tablespoons butter
2 tablespoons flour
1/4 tablespoon salt
Dash pepper
1 cup milk
1 cup cooked, flaked walleye, yellow perch or other fish
1/3 cup celery, chopped
1/4 cup bread crumbs

Cut green peppers in half, remove seeds and set aside. Melt butter in a saucepan over low heat. Mix in flour, salt and a dash of pepper. Add milk. Cook over moderate heat, stirring constantly, until mixture thickens. Remove from heat and add fish and celery. Pour mixture into halved green peppers. Top with bread crumbs. Bake at 400 degrees F for 15 minutes. Yield: 4 servings.

Nutrition Facts

Serving Size 229 g

Amount Per Serving

Calories 272	Calories from Fat 130
	% Daily Value*
Total Fat 14.5g	22%
Saturated Fat 6.2g	31%
Cholesterol 40mg	13%
Sodium 865mg	36%
Total Carbohydrates 24.4g	8%
Dietary Fiber 2.2g	9%
Sugars 5.7g	
Protein 12.5g	
Vitamin A 11%	Vitamin C 111%
Calcium 4%	Iron 11%

Nutrition Grade B-
* Based on a 2000 calorie diet

Fish-Stuffed Tomatoes

4 firm tomatoes
1 cup cooked white bass, freshwater drum or other fish
1 hard-boiled egg, chopped
1/8 teaspoon salt
1/8 teaspoon pepper
1/4 cup buttered bread crumbs
1/4 cup grated cheese

Cut the top slice from each tomato and scoop out pulp. Mix tomato pulp with flaked fish, chopped egg, salt and pepper. Fill tomatoes with fish mixture. Sprinkle 1 tablespoon bread crumbs and 1 tablespoon cheese on top of each tomato. Place stuffed tomatoes in a baking dish with 1/2 cup water and bake at 375 degrees F for 25 minutes. Yield: 4 servings.

Nutrition Facts

Serving Size 205 g

Amount Per Serving

Calories 226	Calories from Fat 99
	% Daily Value*
Total Fat 11.0g	17%
Saturated Fat 3.6g	18%
Trans Fat 0.0g	
Cholesterol 68mg	23%
Sodium 553mg	23%
Total Carbohydrates 19.7g	7%
Dietary Fiber 2.0g	8%
Sugars 3.9g	
Protein 13.5g	
Vitamin A 23% •	Vitamin C 26%
Calcium 9% •	Iron 12%

Nutrition Grade B
* Based on a 2000 calorie diet

Oriental Fish with Sweet and Sour Vegetables

2 lb. fish fillets, any firm fleshed fish
1 tablespoon lemon juice
1 tablespoon vegetable oil
2 cups julienne cut carrots
1/2 cup onion, thinly sliced
2 tablespoons water
2 cups sliced celery
1/2 cup sliced water chestnuts
1 can pineapple chunks (8 1/4 oz.)
1 1/2 tablespoons brown sugar
3 tablespoons cider vinegar
1 1/2 tablespoons soy sauce
1 1/2 tablespoons cornstarch

Place fish fillets in a skillet with enough boiling water to barely cover them. Add lemon juice. Cover and simmer for 8 to 10 minutes until fish flakes apart easily with a fork.

Meanwhile, heat vegetable oil in another skillet. Add carrots and onions, stir fry for 5 minutes over moderately high heat. Reduce to moderate heat, add water, cover and steam for 4 minutes. Uncover, add celery and water chestnuts, stir fry for two minutes. Add undrained pineapple. Stir sugar, vinegar, soy sauce and cornstarch slowly into skillet while cooking. Stir until sauce coats vegetables and pineapple. Remove fish from liquid, drain well. Serve topped with sweet-sour vegetable mixture. Yield: 4 servings.

Nutrition Facts

Serving Size 510 g

Amount Per Serving

Calories 748	Calories from Fat 287
	% Daily Value*
Total Fat 31.8g	**49%**
Saturated Fat 7.2g	**36%**
Trans Fat 0.0g	
Cholesterol 77mg	**26%**
Sodium 1642mg	**68%**
Total Carbohydrates 82.0g	**27%**
Dietary Fiber 4.5g	**18%**
Sugars 15.9g	
Protein 36.0g	

| Vitamin A 191% | • | Vitamin C 73% |
| Calcium 11% | • | Iron 35% |

Nutrition Grade B

* Based on a 2000 calorie diet

Lake Erie Grill-Out

2 lbs. fish fillets (walleye, smallmouth bass or freshwater drum)
1/2 cup ketchup
1/4 cup vegetable oil
3 tablespoons lemon juice
3 tablespoons liquid smoke
2 tablespoons vinegar
1 tablespoon salt
2 tablespoons Worcestershire sauce
1/2 tablespoon grated onion
1 clove garlic, finely chopped or 1 tablespoon garlic powder
3 drops hot pepper or Tabasco® sauce (optional)

Cut fillets into serving size pieces. Place in single layer in shallow baking dish. In a separate bowl, combine remaining ingredients. Pour half the mixture over fillets and marinade for 45 minutes in refrigerator -- turn once. Remove fish and place in a hinged wire grill. Use the other half of marinade for basting. Cook 4 inches from medium hot coals for 8, basting frequently. Turn, baste again and cook 7 to10 minutes longer or until fish flakes apart easily with a fork. Yield: 6 servings.

Nutrition Facts
Serving Size 209 g

Amount Per Serving

Calories 459	Calories from Fat 250

	% Daily Value*
Total Fat 27.8g	43%
Saturated Fat 6.1g	31%
Trans Fat 0.0g	
Cholesterol 51mg	17%
Sodium 2247mg	94%
Total Carbohydrates 32.1g	11%
Dietary Fiber 0.9g	3%
Sugars 5.8g	
Protein 22.6g	

Vitamin A 5%	Vitamin C 11%
Calcium 3%	Iron 18%

Nutrition Grade C+
* Based on a 2000 calorie diet

Fish Hash

1 cup of cold cooked fish fillets
1 cup cold boiled potatoes
1 large onion, grated
1/4 teaspoon sage
1 egg, beaten
3 tablespoons butter
Minced parsley, green onions or ketchup for serving

Cut the potatoes into small pieces and flake the fish. Add onion, sage and beaten egg. Melt butter in a large frying pan. When hot, press the hash in and cook over medium heat until crusty brown underneath. Invert on to a hot platter and sprinkle to taste with minced parsley, green onions or ketchup. Yield: 2 servings.

Nutrition Facts

Serving Size 307 g

Amount Per Serving

Calories 529	Calories from Fat 302
	% Daily Value*
Total Fat 33.6g	**52%**
Saturated Fat 14.9g	**74%**
Cholesterol 166mg	**55%**
Sodium 764mg	**32%**
Total Carbohydrates 38.3g	**13%**
Dietary Fiber 3.7g	**15%**
Sugars 4.2g	
Protein 21.7g	

Vitamin A 14%	•	Vitamin C 34%
Calcium 6%	•	Iron 19%

Nutrition Grade B-
* Based on a 2000 calorie diet

Freshwater Drum Fillets Italian Style

2 cups onions, chopped
2 cloves garlic, minced
1/4 cup butter
1 can tomato paste (6 oz.)
1 can Italian style tomatoes, undrained (1 lb. 12 oz.)
1/2 teaspoon sugar
1 1/2 tablespoons oregano
1 teaspoon salt
1/4 tablespoon pepper
1/4 cup fresh parsley, chopped
2 lbs. freshwater drum or other fish fillets
1/2 teaspoon salt
1 cup grated Mozzarella cheese
1/4 cup Parmesan cheese

Sauté onion and garlic in butter until tender. Add tomato paste, tomatoes, sugar, oregano, 1 teaspoon salt, and pepper; mix well. Cover and cook on medium-low for 30 minutes, stirring occasionally. Add parsley. Spoon the sauce into the bottom of a 13x9" baking dish; add the fish fillets on top of sauce. Sprinkle with 1/2 teaspoon salt, then Mozzarella cheese and Parmesan cheese. Bake at 400 degrees F for 15 to 20 minutes or until fish flakes apart easily with a fork. Yield: 6 servings.

Nutrition Facts

Serving Size 394 g

Amount Per Serving

Calories 579	Calories from Fat 284
	% Daily Value*
Total Fat 31.5g	**49%**
Saturated Fat 12.3g	**62%**
Trans Fat 0.0g	
Cholesterol 86mg	**29%**
Sodium 3879mg	**162%**
Total Carbohydrates 45.2g	**15%**
Dietary Fiber 4.4g	**18%**
Sugars 10.2g	
Protein 31.9g	
Vitamin A 34% •	Vitamin C 50%
Calcium 28% •	Iron 30%

Nutrition Grade B-

* Based on a 2000 calorie diet

Fish Burgers

1 lb. ground fish
1 tablespoon lemon juice
1/4 cup flour
1/2 teaspoon salt
1/8 teaspoon pepper
1/2 cup vegetable oil
6 split, heated hamburger buns
6 lettuce leaves
2 tablespoons mayonnaise
6 tomato slices

Sprinkle ground fish with lemon juice. Mix flour, salt and pepper. Cover the fish with the flour mixture. Panfry in 1/4" hot oil until burgers are lightly browned. In each bun arrange crisp lettuce, fish patty, mayonnaise and a slice of tomato. Yield: 6 servings.

Nutrition Facts

Serving Size 170 g

Amount Per Serving

Calories 375 — Calories from Fat 199

	% Daily Value*
Total Fat 22.1g	**34%**
Saturated Fat 4.1g	**21%**
Trans Fat 0.0g	
Cholesterol 38mg	**13%**
Sodium 467mg	**19%**
Total Carbohydrates 26.0g	**9%**
Dietary Fiber 1.4g	**6%**
Sugars 3.9g	
Protein 17.8g	

Vitamin A 3% • Vitamin C 5%
Calcium 6% • Iron 12%

Nutrition Grade D+
* Based on a 2000 calorie diet

TROUT RECIPES

Trout

Fruit-Stuffed Grilled Trout

4 pan dressed rainbow trout (6 to 8 ounces each)
2 tablespoons margarine, melted
1 tablespoon lemon juice
Nonstick cooking spray
Fruit stuffing (recipe below)

Fruit stuffing:

1/3 cup diced mixed dried fruit
1 cup seasoned croutons
1 green onion, chopped
2 tablespoons margarine, melted
2 tablespoons dry white wine or apple juice
1/8 teaspoon ground allspice
1/4 teaspoon salt

Combine all ingredients for fruit stuffing and mix until liquid is absorbed. Stuff fish with fruit stuffing, closing any openings with toothpicks, if needed. Spray a wire grill basket with cooking spray. Place fish in basket. Grill basket 5 to 6 inches from medium coals for 12 to 15 minutes turning once, until fish flakes easily with fork. Mix margarine and lemon juice together. Brush the fish occasionally with margarine mixture. Yield: 4 servings.

Nutrition Facts

Serving Size 123 g

Amount Per Serving

Calories 323　　　　Calories from Fat 167

　　　　　　　　　　　　　% Daily Value*

Total Fat 18.6g	**29%**
Saturated Fat 3.3g	**17%**
Cholesterol 47mg	**16%**
Sodium 451mg	**19%**
Total Carbohydrates 21.4g	**7%**
Dietary Fiber 2.3g	**9%**
Sugars 1.4g	
Protein 18.3g	

Vitamin A 22%　　•　　Vitamin C 11%
Calcium 6%　　　•　　Iron 12%

Nutrition Grade B+

* Based on a 2000 calorie diet

Oven-Barbecued Lake Trout

1/2 cup vegetable oil
1 teaspoon salt
Dash pepper
1 clove garlic, minced
1 cup shredded cheddar cheese
1 cup dry bread crumbs
2 lbs. lake trout fillets
1 cup barbecue sauce
Nonstick cooking spray

In shallow bowl, combine oil, salt, pepper and garlic. In another bowl, combine cheese and bread crumbs. Dip trout fillets into oil mixture; then in cheese mixture. Spray a baking pan with cooking spray and arrange fish in pan; top with any remaining cheese-crumb mixture. Bake at 450 degrees F for 7 to 10 minutes. Heat barbecue sauce; pour over fish. Bake 5 minutes longer, until fish flakes easily when tested with fork. Keep remaining sauce hot; serve over fish. Yield: 8 servings.

Nutrition Facts

Serving Size 187 g

Amount Per Serving

Calories 449	Calories from Fat 231
	% Daily Value*
Total Fat 25.7g	**40%**
Saturated Fat 8.2g	**41%**
Trans Fat 0.0g	
Cholesterol 92mg	**31%**
Sodium 906mg	**38%**
Total Carbohydrates 23.8g	**8%**
Dietary Fiber 1.4g	**6%**
Sugars 9.2g	
Protein 30.6g	
Vitamin A 36%	Vitamin C 4%
Calcium 22%	Iron 5%

Nutrition Grade B-
* Based on a 2000 calorie diet

Baked Trout Fillets

1 lb. trout fillets
1/4 cup grated Parmesan cheese
1 tablespoon lemon juice
1 tablespoon onion, chopped
1 cup sour cream
1/2 teaspoon salt
1/8 teaspoon paprika
Nonstick cooking spray

Place fish in a shallow 3-quart baking dish that has been sprayed with cooking spray. In a bowl, combine the Parmesan cheese, lemon juice, onion, sour cream and salt; spread mixture over fish. Sprinkle with paprika. Bake, uncovered, at 350 degrees F for 20 to 25 minutes or until fish flakes easily when tested with fork. Yield: 4 servings.

Nutrition Facts

Serving Size 184 g

Amount Per Serving

Calories 368	Calories from Fat 211
	% Daily Value*
Total Fat 23.5g	36%
Saturated Fat 10.3g	51%
Cholesterol 115mg	38%
Sodium 494mg	21%
Total Carbohydrates 3.1g	1%
Protein 34.5g	
Vitamin A 10% • Vitamin C 5%	
Calcium 20% • Iron 13%	

Nutrition Grade B
* Based on a 2000 calorie diet

Broiled Trout Kabobs

8 trout fillets
1 cup chili sauce
1/3 cup vegetable oil
1/4 cup lemon juice
2 tablespoons brown sugar
2 teaspoons celery salt
1/8 teaspoon Tabasco® sauce

Remove skins and bones from trout and cut into 1 inch cubes. Combine remaining ingredients to make a sauce. Reserve 1/4 cup of sauce in refrigerator. Marinate trout cubes in remainder of sauce for several hours in refrigerator, then drain and thread on skewers. Broil over coals or in broiler, turning and basting occasionally with reserved sauce, until trout flakes easily when tested with a fork, about 10 minutes. Yield: 8 servings.

Nutrition Facts

Serving Size 111 g

Amount Per Serving

Calories 212	Calories from Fat 131
	% Daily Value*
Total Fat 14.5g	22%
Saturated Fat 2.8g	14%
Cholesterol 46mg	15%
Sodium 808mg	34%
Total Carbohydrates 2.9g	1%
Sugars 2.7g	
Protein 16.7g	
Vitamin A 2%	Vitamin C 42%
Calcium 4%	Iron 8%

Nutrition Grade B+

* Based on a 2000 calorie diet

Lemon Butter Trout

4 medium trout, with heads if desired
3 tablespoons butter, melted
Juice of 2 lemons
1/2 teaspoon seasoned salt
1/8 teaspoon seasoned pepper
1 large onion, sliced thin and divided into rings

Place fish in broiler pan. Sprinkle outside skin and inside cavity with seasoned salt and pepper. Mix the melted butter and lemon juice together and drizzle butter mixture over fish. Broil for 5 to 6 minutes, then flip the fish over. Scatter the raw rings of onion over top of fish. Broil for 5 to 6 minutes more, until trout flakes easily when tested with a fork. Yield: 4 servings.

Nutrition Facts

Serving Size 112 g

Amount Per Serving

Calories 210	Calories from Fat 125
	% Daily Value*
Total Fat 13.9g	**21%**
Saturated Fat 6.4g	**32%**
Cholesterol 69mg	**23%**
Sodium 295mg	**12%**
Total Carbohydrates 3.6g	**1%**
Dietary Fiber 0.7g	**3%**
Sugars 1.6g	
Protein 17.0g	

Vitamin A 6%	Vitamin C 6%
Calcium 5%	Iron 7%

Nutrition Grade B
* Based on a 2000 calorie diet

Easy Trout Patties

1 1/2 cups cooked, flaked trout
1/2 tablespoon salt
1 egg
1 1/2 cups mashed potatoes (instant potatoes may be substituted)
1 tablespoon onion, minced
1 tablespoon parsley flakes
1/8 teaspoon salt
1/8 teaspoon pepper
1/4 cup vegetable oil
1/2 cup flour
4 wheat hamburger buns

Combine all ingredients except vegetable oil and flour. Shape into 4 patties and roll in flour. Heat oil in skillet. Cook the patties for 3 minutes on each side or until browned. Drain on paper towels. Yield: 4 servings.

Nutrition Facts

Serving Size 242 g

Amount Per Serving

Calories 519 — Calories from Fat 193

	% Daily Value*
Total Fat 21.4g	33%
Saturated Fat 4.1g	20%
Trans Fat 0.0g	
Cholesterol 73mg	24%
Sodium 1496mg	62%
Total Carbohydrates 60.0g	20%
Dietary Fiber 2.5g	10%
Sugars 5.2g	
Protein 22.1g	

Vitamin A 4% • Vitamin C 5%
Calcium 5% • Iron 16%

Nutrition Grade B
* Based on a 2000 calorie diet

Wine Poached Trout

2 rainbow trout
1/2 teaspoon dill seeds
1/4 teaspoon rosemary
1/8 teaspoon seasoning salt
1/2 cup dry white wine
2 cups salad greens

Clean trout and remove heads, tails and fins. Add seasonings to wine and poach (gently simmer) trout in wine mixture for 15 to 20 minutes or until fish is cooked through. Remove skin using a very sharp knife and lift fillets from bones. Serve trout on crisp salad greens. Yield: 2 servings.

Nutrition Facts

Serving Size 177 g

Amount Per Serving

Calories 177	Calories from Fat 49
	% Daily Value*
Total Fat 5.4g	8%
Saturated Fat 0.9g	5%
Cholesterol 46mg	15%
Sodium 197mg	8%
Total Carbohydrates 3.6g	1%
Dietary Fiber 0.8g	3%
Sugars 1.6g	
Protein 17.1g	
Vitamin A 6%	Vitamin C 3%
Calcium 6%	Iron 10%

Nutrition Grade B
* Based on a 2000 calorie diet

Baked Trout Surprise

4 trout fillets
1/2 cup onion, diced
1 cup celery, diced
1/2 cup red or green bell pepper, diced
3/4 cup crabmeat (can use fake)
1 cup bread crumbs
1/4 cup margarine (divided)
2 garlic cloves, crushed
1 teaspoon salt
1/2 teaspoon cayenne pepper
1 egg
1 lemon for garnish (1/2 drizzle over fish as it broils)
1/8 teaspoon salt
1/8 teaspoon pepper
1/4 teaspoon paprika
Nonstick cooking spray

Wash the trout with cold water; pat dry. Lightly salt and pepper fish. Put onion, celery and bell pepper in a small bowl and mix with the crab meat, bread crumbs and 1/2 of the margarine; add garlic and other seasonings, then add the egg to this stuffing mixture.

Spray a baking dish with cooking spray; stuff the trout with the crabmeat bread mixture and line the fish up in the baking pan. Sprinkle with paprika, salt and pepper. Bake at 350 degrees F for 45 minutes. Baste with remaining margarine. The last 10 minutes, put fish under the broiler and brown lightly. Yield: 4 servings.

Nutrition Facts

Serving Size 230 g

Amount Per Serving

Calories 413   Calories from Fat 176

	% Daily Value*
Total Fat 19.5g	**30%**
Saturated Fat 3.6g	**18%**
Cholesterol 98mg	**33%**
Sodium 1543mg	**64%**
Total Carbohydrates 31.8g	**11%**
Dietary Fiber 2.6g	**10%**
Sugars 7.0g	
Protein 26.6g	

| Vitamin A 25% | • | Vitamin C 30% |
| Calcium 12% | • | Iron 18% |

Nutrition Grade A-

* Based on a 2000 calorie diet

Grilled Rainbow Trout

2 pounds rainbow trout fillets
1/8 cup vegetable oil
1/2 teaspoon paprika
1/2 cup margarine, melted
2 tablespoons lemon juice
2 tablespoons lime juice
Lemon wedges

Generously grease grill or hinged wire grill basket. Brush fillets with vegetable oil. Sprinkle with paprika. Mix margarine, lemon juice and lime juice. Grill fish 3 to 4 inches from medium coals for 5 to 7 minutes, turning once and brushing frequently with margarine mixture, until fish flakes easily with fork. Serve with lemon wedges. Yield: 6 servings.

Nutrition Facts

Serving Size 195 g

Amount Per Serving

Calories 468	Calories from Fat 293
	% Daily Value*
Total Fat 32.6g	50%
Saturated Fat 5.6g	28%
Cholesterol 112mg	37%
Sodium 280mg	12%
Total Carbohydrates 1.7g	1%
Protein 40.6g	

Vitamin A 17%	•	Vitamin C 17%
Calcium 9%	•	Iron 17%

Nutrition Grade B+

* Based on a 2000 calorie diet

Smoked Trout Spread

1 lb. smoked trout
1/2 lb. cream cheese
2 oz. butter, softened
1/4 cup heavy cream
1 tablespoon horseradish

Combine and mix all ingredients with a hand mixer until smooth. Enjoy on crackers, toasted bagels or munchie of your choice. Yield: 10 servings.

NUTRITION FACTS PER SERVING: (TROUT SPREAD ONLY)

Nutrition Facts

Serving Size 78 g

Amount Per Serving

Calories 217	Calories from Fat 157
	% Daily Value*
Total Fat 17.5g	**27%**
Saturated Fat 9.2g	**46%**
Cholesterol 75mg	**25%**
Sodium 136mg	**6%**
Total Carbohydrates 0.8g	**0%**
Protein 13.9g	

| Vitamin A 10% | • | Vitamin C 1% |
| Calcium 5% | • | Iron 6% |

Nutrition Grade B-
* Based on a 2000 calorie diet

PERCH RECIPES

Perch

Chili-Baked Fresh Perch

2 lbs. whole fresh dressed perch
3/4 cup chili sauce
1/4 cup red wine vinegar or red wine
2 tablespoons onion, finely chopped
3/4 cup grated American cheese

Arrange fish in buttered, shallow baking pan. In a bowl, combine chili sauce, wine vinegar and onion. Spread mixture on fish and sprinkle with cheese. Bake at 450 degrees for 15 to 20 minutes, until fish flakes easily when tested with fork. Yield: 6 servings.

Nutrition Facts

Serving Size 207 g

Amount Per Serving

Calories 200	Calories from Fat 58
	% Daily Value*
Total Fat 6.4g	10%
Saturated Fat 2.1g	11%
Trans Fat 0.0g	
Cholesterol 71mg	24%
Sodium 1061mg	44%
Total Carbohydrates 2.0g	1%
Sugars 1.6g	
Protein 30.9g	

Vitamin A 3%	•	Vitamin C 36%
Calcium 22%	•	Iron 10%

Nutrition Grade C+
* Based on a 2000 calorie diet

Caper Butter Fillets

1 lb. perch fillets
3 tablespoons butter

Microwave butter about 30 seconds to melt. Coat fish with butter and arrange fish in a microwavable dish with thickest portions to the outside of the dish. Cover with plastic wrap and microwave on high 5 to 7 minutes, or until fish flakes easily. Let rest about 2 minutes while you prepare the sauce.

Caper Butter Sauce:
1/4 cup butter
1/4 cup parsley, chopped
2 tablespoons capers, crushed
1 teaspoon lemon juice
1/2 teaspoon salt
Dash white pepper

Mix all ingredients together and microwave on high for 1 to 1-1/2 minutes. Drain the cooking liquid from fish, pour sauce over fish and serve. Yield: 4 servings.

Nutrition Facts

Serving Size 148 g

Amount Per Serving

Calories 291	Calories from Fat 200
	% Daily Value*
Total Fat 22.3g	**34%**
Saturated Fat 12.8g	**64%**
Cholesterol 99mg	**33%**
Sodium 654mg	**27%**
Total Carbohydrates 0.5g	**0%**
Protein 21.5g	

Vitamin A 19%	•	Vitamin C 10%
Calcium 11%	•	Iron 8%

Nutrition Grade D
* Based on a 2000 calorie diet

Breaded Lemon Perch

20 round buttery crackers, crushed (1/2 cup)
1/4 teaspoon salt
1/8 teaspoon white pepper
1/4 cup margarine or butter, melted
2 tablespoons lemon juice
1 pound perch fillets, cut into 4 serving pieces
1/2 teaspoon paprika

Mix cracker crumbs, salt and white pepper. In another bowl, mix margarine and lemon juice together. Pat the fillets dry. Dip fish into margarine mixture then coat with cracker crumb mixture. Arrange fish on a microwavable rack in microwavable dish, thickest parts of fish to the outside. Sprinkle with paprika. Microwave, uncovered on high for 5 minutes, rotating dish 1/2 turn after 2 minutes, until fish flakes apart easily when tested with a fork. Yield: 4 servings.

Nutrition Facts

Serving Size 151 g

Amount Per Serving

Calories 291	Calories from Fat 159

	% Daily Value*
Total Fat 17.7g	**27%**
Saturated Fat 1.9g	**10%**
Cholesterol 45mg	**15%**
Sodium 372mg	**16%**
Total Carbohydrates 8.7g	**3%**
Protein 22.2g	

Vitamin A 13%	Vitamin C 6%
Calcium 11%	Iron 7%

Nutrition Grade D+

* Based on a 2000 calorie diet

Perch-Stuffed Baked Potatoes

4 large baking potatoes
2 tablespoons olive oil
1 tablespoon butter
2 tablespoons onion, minced
1 cup low-fat hot milk
1/8 teaspoon salt
1/8 teaspoon pepper
1 lb. perch, cooked and flaked
1 cup grated cheese

Preheat oven to 425 degrees F. Scrub the potatoes, rub the potatoes all over with a little olive oil and prick each potato with a fork a few times. Bake potatoes at 425 degrees F, for 50 to 60 minutes, or until soft.

Slice off the tops of each potato and scoop out insides, leaving shells intact with about 1/4 inch of potato left on the skin. Mash insides with butter, onion, hot milk and salt and pepper. Stir in fish, stuff mixture back into shells and sprinkle with cheese. Bake at 375 degrees F for 15 to 20 minutes, or until cheese melts. Yield: 4 servings.

Nutrition Facts

Serving Size 518 g

Amount Per Serving

Calories 582	Calories from Fat 194
	% Daily Value*
Total Fat 21.6g	**33%**
Saturated Fat 9.5g	**48%**
Cholesterol 171mg	**57%**
Sodium 416mg	**17%**
Total Carbohydrates 56.4g	**19%**
Dietary Fiber 4.1g	**17%**
Sugars 5.6g	
Protein 43.4g	
Vitamin A 11%	Vitamin C 95%
Calcium 43%	Iron 21%

Nutrition Grade B+

* Based on a 2000 calorie diet

Fillets with Cheese Sauce

4 slices lean bacon
1 large onion, thinly sliced
2 large tomatoes, thinly sliced
2 lbs. perch fillets
1/8 teaspoon salt
1/8 teaspoon pepper
1 1/2 tablespoons lemon juice
1 can cheddar cheese soup (11 oz.)

Arrange ingredients in layers in a well-greased casserole dish in the following order: bacon, onions, tomatoes, perch fillets. Season with salt, pepper and lemon juice, and spread the undiluted cheese soup over the fillets. Bake at 350 degrees F for 20 minutes or until fish flakes apart easily when tested with a fork. Yield: 6 servings.

Nutrition Facts

Serving Size 305 g

Amount Per Serving

Calories 235	Calories from Fat 61
	% Daily Value*
Total Fat 6.8g	**10%**
Saturated Fat 1.5g	7%
Trans Fat 0.0g	
Cholesterol 66mg	**22%**
Sodium 566mg	**24%**
Total Carbohydrates 10.3g	**3%**
Dietary Fiber 1.7g	7%
Sugars 3.7g	
Protein 30.9g	

Vitamin A 15%	•	Vitamin C 19%
Calcium 17%	•	Iron 10%

Nutrition Grade C+
* Based on a 2000 calorie diet

Baked Fillets in Sour Cream

1 lbs. perch fillets
1 lemon, cut in thin slices
2/3 cup sour cream
1/8 teaspoon salt
1/8 teaspoon pepper
1/4 teaspoon paprika

Preheat oven to 400 degrees F. Cover bottom of shallow baking dish with lemon slices; arrange fish fillets on top. Cover and bake for 30 minutes, or until fish easily flakes with fork, but still moist. Uncover and spread with sour cream and salt combined. Sprinkle with pepper and paprika. Continue cooking just until sour cream is lightly browned, about 10 minutes. Yield: 4 servings.

Nutrition Facts

Serving Size 167 g

Amount Per Serving

Calories 187	Calories from Fat 82
	% Daily Value*
Total Fat 9.1g	14%
Saturated Fat 5.0g	25%
Trans Fat 0.0g	
Cholesterol 117mg	39%
Sodium 160mg	7%
Total Carbohydrates 3.1g	1%
Protein 22.5g	

Vitamin A 6%	•	Vitamin C 14%
Calcium 13%	•	Iron 9%

Nutrition Grade C-
* Based on a 2000 calorie diet

Yellow Perch with Mushroom Sauce

2 lbs. yellow perch
3 tablespoons butter (divided)
2 tablespoons lemon juice
1 tablespoon salt
3 strips bacon
1/4 cup onion, chopped
1 clove garlic, minced
1/2 cup sliced mushrooms, fresh or canned
1 tablespoon flour
1/4 cup ketchup
1/4 cup dry white wine (optional)
1/4 cup water

Arrange fish fillets in a greased baking pan in a single layer. Drizzle 2 tablespoons melted butter and lemon juice over fish. Sprinkle with salt. Broil for about 5 minutes on each side approximately 4 inches away from heat source. Broil until fish flakes apart easily with a fork.

Meanwhile, fry bacon and drain on paper towels. Add 1 tablespoon butter to bacon drippings and sauté onions and garlic in drippings until tender. Add mushrooms, flour, ketchup, wine and water to bacon drippings. Cook, stirring constantly until sauce is thickened. Spoon sauce over broiled fish. Sprinkle with bacon pieces. Yield: 6 servings.

Nutrition Facts

Serving Size 212 g

Amount Per Serving

Calories 294 — Calories from Fat 97

% Daily Value*

Total Fat 10.8g — **17%**
  Saturated Fat 4.1g — **21%**
  Trans Fat 0.0g
Cholesterol 109mg — **36%**
Sodium 1562mg — **65%**
Total Carbohydrates 4.8g — **2%**
  Sugars 2.8g
Protein 39.6g

Vitamin A 5% • Vitamin C 8%
Calcium 3% • Iron 13%

Nutrition Grade F

* Based on a 2000 calorie diet

Yellow Perch Burgers

1 1/2 lbs. boneless yellow perch
1 qt. boiling water
1 tablespoon salt
3 eggs, beaten
1/3 cup grated Parmesan cheese
1 tablespoon parsley, chopped
1 clove garlic, finely chopped
1/2 tablespoon salt
Dash pepper
1/2 cup dry bread crumbs
6 toasted hamburger buns
1/4 cup vegetable oil
1/8 cup tartar sauce

Bring 1 quart of water with 1 tablespoon salt added to a boil. Place fish fillets in boiling, salted water. Cover and return to boiling point. Immediately lower heat and simmer for 7 to 10 minutes or until fish flakes apart easily with a fork. Drain and flake fish. In a bowl, mix beaten eggs, cheese, parsley, garlic, 1/2 teaspoon salt and pepper together. Combine with fish. Chill in refrigerator for one hour or longer.

Shape chilled mixture into 6 patties and roll in bread crumbs. Fry in hot oil at medium heat to brown both sides. Turn only once. Cook the patties for 3 minutes on each side or until browned. Drain on paper towels. Serve on buns with tartar sauce. Yield: 5 servings.

Nutrition Facts

Serving Size 297 g

Amount Per Serving

Calories 529　　　　Calories from Fat 193

　　　　　　　　　　　　　　　% Daily Value*

Total Fat 21.5g　　　　　　　　　　33%
　Saturated Fat 4.8g　　　　　　　　24%
Cholesterol 185mg　　　　　　　　62%
Sodium 2714mg　　　　　　　　　113%
Total Carbohydrates 34.0g　　　　11%
　Dietary Fiber 1.6g　　　　　　　　　6%
　Sugars 4.2g
Protein 46.3g

Vitamin A 4%　　•　　Vitamin C 2%
Calcium 20%　　•　　Iron 26%

Nutrition Grade C+

* Based on a 2000 calorie diet

Oven Fried Perch Fillets

2 lb. frozen perch fillets, thawed
1/2 cup fine dry bread crumbs
1 teaspoon paprika
1 tablespoon parsley
1 teaspoon salt
1/8 teaspoon pepper
2 tablespoons oil
Nonstick cooking spray

Separate fillets carefully. In a bowl, combine bread crumbs, paprika, parsley, salt and pepper. Add oil and mix with a fork until thoroughly mixed. Spread crumb mixture on wax paper. Press fillets into crumbs, coating both sides. Put fish on a baking sheet sprayed with cooking spray. Bake at 450 degrees F for 12 minutes or until fish flakes easily when tested with fork. Yield: 6 servings.

Nutrition Facts

Serving Size 168 g

Amount Per Serving

Calories 227	Calories from Fat 71
	% Daily Value*
Total Fat 7.9g	12%
Saturated Fat 0.7g	4%
Trans Fat 0.0g	
Cholesterol 60mg	20%
Sodium 684mg	29%
Total Carbohydrates 7.1g	2%
Dietary Fiber 0.7g	3%
Sugars 0.6g	
Protein 29.6g	
Vitamin A 5%	Vitamin C 2%
Calcium 15%	Iron 12%

Nutrition Grade C
* Based on a 2000 calorie diet

CATFISH RECIPES

Catfish

Baked Catfish with Rice

2 lbs. catfish fillets
1/3 cup bell pepper, chopped
2 tablespoons fresh parsley, chopped
1 tablespoon lemon juice
1/2 teaspoon salt
1/2 teaspoon cayenne pepper
1/2 cup onion, chopped
1 clove garlic, crushed
1 can whole tomatoes, undrained and chopped (28 oz.)
4 cups cooked white rice

Cut the fish into 8 serving size pieces. Place fish in 13 x 9 inch baking dish. Combine bell pepper, parsley, lemon juice, salt, cayenne pepper, onion, garlic and tomatoes. Pour over fish.

Bake uncovered at 450 degrees F for 25 to 30 minutes or until fish flakes easily with fork. Spoon tomato mixture over fish occasionally. Serve over rice. Yield: 8 servings.

Nutrition Facts

Serving Size 251 g

Amount Per Serving

Calories 267	Calories from Fat 79
	% Daily Value*
Total Fat 8.8g	14%
Saturated Fat 1.7g	8%
Cholesterol 53mg	18%
Sodium 416mg	17%
Total Carbohydrates 24.4g	8%
Dietary Fiber 1.4g	5%
Sugars 4.5g	
Protein 20.3g	
Vitamin A 18% •	Vitamin C 26%
Calcium 5% •	Iron 19%

Nutrition Grade A-
* Based on a 2000 calorie diet

Fish Creole

1 can stewed tomatoes (8 oz.)
1 teaspoon Kitchen Bouquet®
1/4 teaspoon sugar
1/4 teaspoon thyme, crumbled
1/4 teaspoon curry powder
1 pound catfish
Parsley (optional)
1/8 teaspoon salt

Combine tomatoes, Kitchen Bouquet®, sugar, thyme and curry powder, breaking up large tomato pieces with spoon. Cut fish into 4 portions. Place in shallow baking pan. Spoon tomato mixture over top of fish. Cover pan with lid or foil. Bake at 450 degrees F for 15 minutes or until fish flakes with fork. Sprinkle with minced parsley, if desired. Sprinkle with salt. Serve with rice, spooning pan juices over. Yield: 4 servings.

Nutrition Facts

Serving Size 196 g

Amount Per Serving

Calories 287	Calories from Fat 141
	% Daily Value*
Total Fat 15.7g	**24%**
Saturated Fat 3.9g	**19%**
Trans Fat 0.0g	
Cholesterol 92mg	**31%**
Sodium 620mg	**26%**
Total Carbohydrates 14.1g	**5%**
Dietary Fiber 1.4g	**5%**
Sugars 3.2g	
Protein 21.2g	
Vitamin A 8% •	Vitamin C 7%
Calcium 7% •	Iron 12%

Nutrition Grade C+
* Based on a 2000 calorie diet

Catfish Stew

2 medium onions, sliced
1 clove garlic, finely chopped
2 teaspoons chili powder
2 teaspoons vegetable oil
1 can whole tomatoes, undrained (28 oz.)
1 3/4 cups water
1/2 cup uncooked regular long grain rice
1/2 teaspoon dried oregano leaves
1/2 teaspoon dried thyme leaves
1/2 teaspoon ground cumin
1/2 teaspoon red pepper sauce
1 package frozen sliced okra (10 oz.)
1 pound catfish fillets, cut into 1 inch pieces
1/2 cup green bell pepper, chopped

Cook onions, garlic and chili powder in the oil in nonstick Dutch oven over medium heat 2 to 3 minutes, stirring frequently, until onions are tender. Stir in tomatoes, water, rice, oregano, thyme, cumin and pepper sauce; break up tomatoes. Heat to boiling; reduce heat. Cover and simmer 20 minutes. Rinse okra with cold water to separate; drain. Stir okra, fillets and bell pepper into tomato mixture. Heat to boiling; reduce heat. Cover and simmer 5 to 10 minutes, stirring occasionally, until fish flakes easily with fork and okra is done. Yield: 6 servings.

Nutrition Facts

Serving Size 387 g

Amount Per Serving

Calories 235	Calories from Fat 70

	% Daily Value*
Total Fat 7.8g	**12%**
Saturated Fat 1.5g	**7%**
Trans Fat 0.0g	
Cholesterol 36mg	**12%**
Sodium 370mg	**15%**
Total Carbohydrates 25.5g	**8%**
Dietary Fiber 3.9g	**16%**
Sugars 6.8g	
Protein 15.7g	

Vitamin A 31%	•	Vitamin C 50%
Calcium 12%	•	Iron 16%

Nutrition Grade A
* Based on a 2000 calorie diet

Blackened Catfish

4 catfish fillets (8 oz. each)
3/4 cup butter, melted
1 tablespoon white pepper
1 tablespoon black pepper
1 teaspoon garlic powder
1 teaspoon salt
1 tablespoon paprika
1 teaspoon cayenne pepper
1/4 teaspoon thyme
1/4 teaspoon oregano
1/4 teaspoon dill
1 teaspoon chili powder

Heat a cast-iron skillet or nonstick pan over medium-high heat for about 8 minutes. Dip each catfish fillet in the melted butter and sprinkle both sides of fillet with a mixture of the white pepper, black pepper, garlic powder, salt, paprika, red pepper, thyme, oregano, dill and chili powder. Place the fillets in the preheated skillet. Drizzle with 2 tablespoons of the melted butter. Cook for 4 to 5 minutes on each side or until blackened, and fish flakes easily with fork. The cooking time will vary depending on the thickness of the fillets.

(Note: Blackened is a technique in quick high heat cooking. It is the seasonings that will blacken, so be careful not to overcook the fillets.) Yield: 4 servings.

Nutrition Facts

Serving Size 211 g

Amount Per Serving

Calories 541　　　　Calories from Fat 425

　　　　　　　　　　　　　　　% Daily Value*

Total Fat 47.2g	**73%**
Saturated Fat 24.2g	**121%**
Cholesterol 167mg	**56%**
Sodium 920mg	**38%**
Total Carbohydrates 4.3g	**1%**
Dietary Fiber 2.0g	**8%**
Sugars 0.5g	
Protein 26.1g	
Vitamin A 49% ·	Vitamin C 7%
Calcium 5% ·	Iron 16%

Nutrition Grade C+

* Based on a 2000 calorie diet

Stuffed Catfish

8 fresh mushrooms, sliced
1/2 onion, chopped
2 shallots, chopped
1/4 cup butter or margarine
8 catfish fillets
1 green bell pepper, finely chopped
1 pimento, finely chopped
1 egg
1/2 cup mayonnaise
1 tablespoon English mustard or spicy brown mustard
1/2 teaspoon salt
1/4 teaspoon white pepper
2 pounds lump crab meat
White wine (5 oz.)
1/4 teaspoon salt
1/8 teaspoon pepper

Sauté the mushrooms, onion and shallots in the butter in a skillet. Spoon into a shallow baking dish. Arrange the fillets in the baking dish on top of the butter mixture. Mix the green pepper, pimento, egg, mayonnaise, mustard, 1/2 teaspoon salt and the white pepper in a bowl. Stir in the crab meat gently. Spoon into a mound on each fillet. Add the wine. Sprinkle with salt and black pepper. Bake at 400 degrees F for 15 to 20 minutes or until the fish flakes easily. Yield: 8 servings.

Nutrition Facts

Serving Size 378 g

Amount Per Serving

Calories 453	Calories from Fat 297
	% Daily Value*
Total Fat 33.0g	51%
Saturated Fat 6.8g	34%
Cholesterol 179mg	60%
Sodium 1103mg	46%
Total Carbohydrates 9.9g	3%
Dietary Fiber 1.2g	5%
Sugars 3.1g	
Protein 43.6g	
Vitamin A 26%	Vitamin C 68%
Calcium 40%	Iron 20%

Nutrition Grade C

* Based on a 2000 calorie diet

SAUCES & COATINGS FOR FISH

Sauces and Coatings

Hollandaise Sauce for Fish

1/4 cup butter
1 teaspoon flour
2 egg yolks, well beaten
3/4 cup boiling water
Juice of 1 lemon
1/4 teaspoon salt
1/8 teaspoon paprika
1/8 teaspoon cayenne pepper

Mix butter and flour smoothly. Put in double boiler. Add egg yolks. Add boiling water and keep stirring until sufficiently thick. When ready to serve, add lemon juice, salt, paprika and pepper. Serve hot. Yield: 2/3 cup sauce.

Nutrition Facts

Serving Size 27 g

Amount Per Serving

Calories 53 — Calories from Fat 50

	% Daily Value*
Total Fat 5.5g	8%
Saturated Fat 3.2g	16%
Cholesterol 54mg	18%
Sodium 93mg	4%
Total Carbohydrates 0.4g	0%
Protein 0.6g	

Vitamin A 4% • Vitamin C 0%
Calcium 1% • Iron 1%

Nutrition Grade C-
* Based on a 2000 calorie diet

Tartar Sauce

2/3 cup mayonnaise or salad dressing
3 tablespoons pickle relish
2 tablespoons stuffed olives, chopped
1 tablespoon grated onion
1 teaspoon prepared horseradish

Add pickle relish, chopped stuffed olives, grated onion and prepared horseradish to mayonnaise or salad dressing. Yield: 1 cup sauce.

NUTRITION FACTS PER SERVING: (SERVING SIZE BASED ON 1 TABLESPOON OF SAUCE)

Nutrition Facts	
Serving Size 15 g	
Amount Per Serving	
Calories 45	Calories from Fat 32
	% Daily Value*
Total Fat 3.6g	6%
Saturated Fat 0.5g	3%
Trans Fat 0.0g	
Cholesterol 3mg	1%
Sodium 129mg	5%
Total Carbohydrates 3.4g	1%
Sugars 1.5g	
Protein 0.1g	
Vitamin A 1% •	Vitamin C 0%
Calcium 0% •	Iron 0%
Nutrition Grade D	
* Based on a 2000 calorie diet	

Garlic Sauce for Fried Fish

6 garlic cloves
1/2 cup vinegar
1 cup olive oil
3 medium potatoes, cooked and mashed
1/8 teaspoon salt
1/8 teaspoon pepper

Crush garlic in a mortar. Add mashed potatoes. Pound well until blended into a paste. Add vinegar and olive oil alternately in very small quantities using an electric mixer. Add salt and pepper; continue beating until sauce is stiff enough to shape. Serve on boiled or fried fish. Yield: 4 1/2 cups.

NUTRITION FACTS PER SERVING: (SERVING SIZE BASED ON 1/4 CUP)

Nutrition Facts

Serving Size 55 g

Amount Per Serving

Calories 123	Calories from Fat 101
	% Daily Value*
Total Fat 11.2g	17%
Saturated Fat 1.6g	8%
Trans Fat 0.0g	
Cholesterol 0mg	0%
Sodium 18mg	1%
Total Carbohydrates 6.0g	2%
Dietary Fiber 0.9g	3%
Protein 0.7g	

Vitamin A 0%	•	Vitamin C 12%
Calcium 1%	•	Iron 1%

Nutrition Grade C
* Based on a 2000 calorie diet

Remoulade Sauce

1 cup mayonnaise
1 hardboiled egg, diced
2 dill pickles, diced
1 tablespoon capers, chopped
1 tablespoon onions, chopped
1/2 teaspoon dry dill
1 teaspoon spicy brown mustard
1 tablespoon lemon juice

Mix all ingredients together and serve with fish. Keep refrigerated. Yield: 1 1/2 cups.

NUTRITION FACTS PER SERVING: (SERVING SIZE BASED ON 1 TABLESPOON OF SAUCE)

Nutrition Facts

Serving Size 19 g

Amount Per Serving

Calories 42 — Calories from Fat 31

	% Daily Value*
Total Fat 3.5g	5%
Saturated Fat 0.6g	3%
Cholesterol 9mg	3%
Sodium 154mg	6%
Total Carbohydrates 2.5g	1%
Sugars 0.7g	
Protein 0.4g	

Vitamin A 1%	•	Vitamin C 1%	
Calcium 0%	•	Iron 1%	

Nutrition Grade D
* Based on a 2000 calorie diet

Basting Sauce for Fish

1 chicken bouillon cube
1/2 cup boiling water
1 cup butter, melted
1/4 teaspoon salt
2 tablespoons lemon juice
1 teaspoon soy sauce
1/2 teaspoon Worcestershire sauce
1 teaspoon paprika

Dissolve chicken bouillon cube in boiling water. Add rest of ingredients. Pour over fish and baste while grilling. Yield: 1 1/2 cups.

NUTRITION FACTS PER SERVING: (SERVING SIZE BASED ON 1 TABLESPOON OF SAUCE)

Nutrition Facts

Serving Size 16 g

Amount Per Serving

Calories 69	Calories from Fat 69
	% Daily Value*
Total Fat 7.7g	12%
Saturated Fat 4.9g	24%
Trans Fat 0.0g	
Cholesterol 20mg	7%
Sodium 117mg	5%
Total Carbohydrates 0.2g	0%
Protein 0.1g	
Vitamin A 6% •	Vitamin C 1%
Calcium 0% •	Iron 0%

Nutrition Grade F
* Based on a 2000 calorie diet

Green Sauce for Fish

1/2 cup fresh minced parsley
2 teaspoons olive oil
2 teaspoons rice/wine vinegar
2 teaspoons spicy brown mustard
1 large or 2 small crushed garlic cloves
1 teaspoon lemon juice
2 anchovies, optional

Put all ingredients in blender. Whiz on "grate" for 10 seconds. Pour over fish fillets. Yield: 6 servings.

NUTRITION FACTS PER SERVING: (SERVING SIZE BASED ON 2 TABLESPOONS OF SAUCE)

Nutrition Facts

Serving Size 53 g

Amount Per Serving

Calories 36 Calories from Fat 20

	% Daily Value*
Total Fat 2.3g	3%
Trans Fat 0.0g	
Cholesterol 6mg	2%
Sodium 311mg	13%
Total Carbohydrates 1.9g	1%
Protein 2.2g	

Vitamin A 8%	•	Vitamin C 12%
Calcium 2%	•	Iron 3%

Nutrition Grade B
* Based on a 2000 calorie diet

Raspberry Zinfandel Butter

1 cup raspberry wine vinegar
1 cup Zinfandel raspberry wine
4 small shallots, minced
1 garlic clove, minced
2 lbs. butter, softened

Bring raspberry wine vinegar to a boil. Add wine, shallots and garlic. Let boil until reduced to 1 cup. Cool. Whip together butter and wine mixture until consistency is smooth. Place in plastic or glass container; refrigerate. To Use: Broil fish. Place 1 ounce portion of butter mixture on top. Allow butter to melt partially over entree before serving. Yield: 48 1 oz. servings.

NUTRITION FACTS PER SERVING: (SERVING SIZE BASED ON 1 OUNCE OF SAUCE)

Nutrition Facts

Serving Size 24 g

Amount Per Serving

Calories 138	Calories from Fat 138
	% Daily Value*
Total Fat 15.3g	24%
Saturated Fat 9.7g	49%
Trans Fat 0.0g	
Cholesterol 41mg	14%
Sodium 109mg	5%
Total Carbohydrates 0.2g	0%
Protein 0.2g	

Vitamin A 10%	•	Vitamin C 0%
Calcium 0%	•	Iron 0%

Nutrition Grade D-
* Based on a 2000 calorie diet

Sesame Marinade

1/4 cup soy sauce
1/4 cup vegetable oil
1/4 cup sesame oil
3 tablespoons lemon juice
1 clove garlic, minced
2 teaspoons sesame seeds

Combine all ingredients and marinate fish in refrigerator in the liquid for a few hours. Remove from marinade; sprinkle fish with sesame seeds. Broil fish for 10 to 20 minutes until opaque. Yield: 3/4 cup.

NUTRITION FACTS PER SERVING: (SERVING SIZE BASED ON 1 TABLESPOON OF SAUCE)

Nutrition Facts

Serving Size 19 g

Amount Per Serving

Calories 87	Calories from Fat 84
	% Daily Value*
Total Fat 9.4g	14%
Saturated Fat 1.6g	8%
Cholesterol 0mg	0%
Sodium 300mg	13%
Total Carbohydrates 0.7g	0%
Protein 0.5g	
Vitamin A 0%	Vitamin C 3%
Calcium 1%	Iron 1%

Nutrition Grade D
* Based on a 2000 calorie diet

Almond Butter

1/4 cup almonds, thinly sliced or slivered
1/4 cup butter

Combine almonds with butter and microwave on high 2 to 3 minutes. Spoon over cooked, drained fillets. Yield: 1/2 cup.

NUTRITION FACTS PER SERVING: (SERVING SIZE BASED ON 1 TABLESPOON OF SAUCE)

Nutrition Facts

Serving Size 10 g

Amount Per Serving

Calories 68	Calories from Fat 65
	% Daily Value*
Total Fat 7.2g	**11%**
Saturated Fat 3.8g	**19%**
Trans Fat 0.0g	
Cholesterol 15mg	**5%**
Sodium 41mg	**2%**
Total Carbohydrates 0.6g	**0%**
Protein 0.7g	

Vitamin A 4%	Vitamin C 0%
Calcium 1%	Iron 1%

Nutrition Grade D+
* Based on a 2000 calorie diet

Beer Batter for Fish

1 cup flour
1 teaspoon baking powder
1 teaspoon salt
2 eggs
1 cup beer
1/4 cup milk

Mix first three ingredients together. Add egg and then beer. Stir well. Dip fish in batter and fry in hot grease (375 degrees F) until golden brown. Yield: 6 servings.

NUTRITION FACTS PER SERVING: (SERVING SIZE BASED ON 1 TABLESPOON OF SAUCE ONLY)

Nutrition Facts

Serving Size 87 g

Amount Per Serving

Calories 120	Calories from Fat 17
	% Daily Value*
Total Fat 1.9g	3%
Saturated Fat 0.6g	3%
Cholesterol 55mg	18%
Sodium 415mg	17%
Total Carbohydrates 18.3g	6%
Dietary Fiber 0.6g	2%
Sugars 0.7g	
Protein 4.5g	
Vitamin A 1%	Vitamin C 0%
Calcium 5%	Iron 7%

Nutrition Grade C+
* Based on a 2000 calorie diet

Lemon Butter

2 tablespoons lemon juice
1 tablespoon grated lemon peel (optional)
1/4 cup butter
1/8 teaspoon Tabasco sauce

Combine lemon juice, lemon peel, butter and Tabasco sauce. Microwave on high 1 to 1 1/2 minutes. Spoon over cooked, drained fillets. Yield: 6 tablespoons.

NUTRITION FACTS PER SERVING: (SERVING SIZE BASED ON 1 TABLESPOON OF SAUCE)

Nutrition Facts

Serving Size 17 g

Amount Per Serving

Calories 70	Calories from Fat 69
	% Daily Value*
Total Fat 7.7g	12%
Saturated Fat 4.9g	25%
Cholesterol 20mg	7%
Sodium 56mg	2%
Total Carbohydrates 0.3g	0%
Protein 0.1g	
Vitamin A 5%	Vitamin C 6%
Calcium 0%	Iron 0%

Nutrition Grade D

* Based on a 2000 calorie diet

White Wine and Garlic

1/4 cup butter
2 tablespoons white wine
1 garlic clove, crushed
1/2 teaspoon salt
1/8 teaspoon white pepper

Combine butter, wine, garlic clove, salt and pepper. Microwave on high 1 to 1 1/2 minutes and spoon over cooked, drained fillets. Yield: 6 tablespoons.

NUTRITION FACTS PER SERVING: (SERVING SIZE BASED ON 1 TABLESPOON OF SAUCE)

Nutrition Facts

Serving Size 15 g

Amount Per Serving

Calories 73 — Calories from Fat 69

	% Daily Value*
Total Fat 7.7g	12%
Saturated Fat 4.9g	24%
Cholesterol 20mg	7%
Sodium 249mg	10%
Total Carbohydrates 0.3g	0%
Protein 0.1g	

Vitamin A 5%	•	Vitamin C 0%
Calcium 0%	•	Iron 0%

Nutrition Grade F
* Based on a 2000 calorie diet

Herbed Butter

1/4 cup butter
2 teaspoons chopped fresh herbs: dill, chives, basil or parsley

Combine butter and chopped herbs. Microwave on high 1 to 1 1/2 minutes. Spoon over cooked, drained fillets. Yield: 4 tablespoons.

NUTRITION FACTS PER SERVING: (SERVING SIZE BASED ON 1 TABLESPOON OF SAUCE)

Nutrition Facts

Serving Size 15 g

Amount Per Serving

Calories 102	Calories from Fat 102
	% Daily Value*
Total Fat 11.5g	**18%**
Saturated Fat 7.3g	**36%**
Cholesterol 31mg	**10%**
Sodium 82mg	**3%**
Total Carbohydrates 0.1g	**0%**
Protein 0.1g	
Vitamin A 8% •	Vitamin C 1%
Calcium 0% •	Iron 0%

Nutrition Grade F
* Based on a 2000 calorie diet

Bacon and Green Onion

3 slices cooked bacon, chopped into pieces
1 1/2 tablespoons green onion, chopped
1 small tomato, seeded and chopped
1/4 cup butter
1 tablespoon lemon juice
1/2 teaspoon salt
1/8 teaspoon pepper

Combine bacon, green onion, tomato, butter, lemon juice, salt and pepper. Microwave on high 1 to 2 minutes. Spoon over cooked, drained fillets. Yield: 2/3 cup.

NUTRITION FACTS PER SERVING: (SERVING SIZE BASED ON 1 TABLESPOON OF SAUCE)

Nutrition Facts

Serving Size 19 g

Amount Per Serving

Calories 53	Calories from Fat 49
	% Daily Value*
Total Fat 5.4g	8%
Saturated Fat 3.2g	16%
Trans Fat 0.0g	
Cholesterol 14mg	5%
Sodium 194mg	8%
Total Carbohydrates 0.5g	0%
Protein 0.9g	

Vitamin A 5%	Vitamin C 3%
Calcium 0%	Iron 0%

Nutrition Grade D-
* Based on a 2000 calorie diet

Shake and Bake for Fish

2 cups cornflakes
3 teaspoons parsley flakes
1 tablespoon paprika
1 teaspoon dry mustard powder
1 teaspoon garlic salt

Crush the cornflakes. Mix all the ingredients together. Coat fish with flour, then dip in an egg white mixed with 1 tablespoon of water, then coat completely with the cornflake mixture. Bake at 425 degrees F for 12 to 15 minutes in a baking pan sprayed with cooking spray, or until fillets are crisp and browned. Yield: Will coat at least 4 fish fillets.

NUTRITION FACTS PER SERVING: (SERVING SIZE BASED ON COATING 1 FISH FILLET)

Nutrition Facts

Serving Size 18 g

Amount Per Serving

Calories 62	Calories from Fat 5
	% Daily Value*
Total Fat 0.6g	1%
Trans Fat 0.0g	
Cholesterol 0mg	0%
Sodium 102mg	4%
Total Carbohydrates 14.0g	5%
Dietary Fiber 1.2g	5%
Sugars 1.9g	
Protein 1.6g	
Vitamin A 25%	Vitamin C 9%
Calcium 1%	Iron 26%

Nutrition Grade A
* Based on a 2000 calorie diet

Cheese Stuffing

1/2 cup onions, sliced
1/4 cup butter or margarine
3/4 teaspoon salt
Dash pepper
1 1/2 cups fresh bread crumbs
1/3 cup grated processed Cheddar cheese

Sauté onions in butter until tender. In a bowl, mix the onions and butter with salt, pepper, bread crumbs and cheese. Use to top 2 lb. cod or haddock fillets or to fill pairs of 1 to 1 1/2 lb. fillets. Yield: 2 1/2 cups.

NUTRITION FACTS PER SERVING: (SERVING SIZE BASED ON 3 TABLESPOONS OF STUFFING)

Nutrition Facts

Serving Size 25 g

Amount Per Serving

Calories 91 — Calories from Fat 43

	% Daily Value*
Total Fat 4.8g	7%
Saturated Fat 2.8g	14%
Cholesterol 12mg	4%
Sodium 302mg	13%
Total Carbohydrates 9.8g	3%
Dietary Fiber 0.6g	3%
Sugars 1.2g	
Protein 2.3g	

Vitamin A 3% • Vitamin C 1%
Calcium 2% • Iron 3%

Nutrition Grade D+
* Based on a 2000 calorie diet

Garden Stuffing

1 small clove garlic
1 teaspoon salt
1/3 cup scallions, minced
1/2 cup green peppers, chopped
1/2 cup celery, chopped
2 tomatoes, peeled, coarsely chopped
3 tablespoons snipped parsley

With a fork, mash garlic with salt in bottom of bowl; add rest of ingredients. Stuffs and tops dressed 6 to 7 lb. fish or several smaller fish. Yield: 2 1/2 cups.

NUTRITION FACTS PER SERVING: (SERVING SIZE BASED ON 3 TABLESPOONS OF STUFFING)

Nutrition Facts
Serving Size 39 g

Amount Per Serving

Calories 7	Calories from Fat 1
	% Daily Value*
Total Fat 0.1g	0%
Trans Fat 0.0g	
Cholesterol 0mg	0%
Sodium 189mg	8%
Total Carbohydrates 1.3g	0%
Sugars 0.7g	
Protein 0.3g	
Vitamin A 6%	Vitamin C 12%
Calcium 1%	Iron 1%

Nutrition Grade A
* Based on a 2000 calorie diet

SIDE DISHES FOR FISH & GAME

Side Dishes for Fish and Game

Pineapple Salad

2 tablespoons sugar
2 tablespoons flour
1 egg, beaten
1 can pineapple chunks, with juice (20 oz.)
2 cups mini marshmallows
1/2 cup pecans

Mix sugar and flour in a bowl. Mix in beaten egg and juice from pineapple. In saucepan, cook mixture for 3 to 4 minutes on high or until mixture thickens, stirring constantly. Add marshmallows and stir until marshmallows dissolve. Add pineapple chunks and nuts. Chill thoroughly before serving. Yield: 4 servings.

Nutrition Facts

Serving Size 197 g

Amount Per Serving

Calories 301 — Calories from Fat 98

% Daily Value*

Total Fat 10.9g	17%
Saturated Fat 1.2g	6%
Trans Fat 0.0g	
Cholesterol 41mg	14%
Sodium 30mg	1%
Total Carbohydrates 48.6g	16%
Dietary Fiber 2.7g	11%
Sugars 39.2g	
Protein 3.8g	

Vitamin A 1% • Vitamin C 86%
Calcium 2% • Iron 6%

Nutrition Grade B-
* Based on a 2000 calorie diet

Wild Rice Casserole

4 cups water
1 cup uncooked wild rice
3/4 cup onion, finely chopped
1/2 cup celery, chopped
2 tablespoons margarine
2 cans mushrooms (4 oz. each)
1 can cream of chicken soup (10.5 oz.)
1 can cream of mushroom soup (10.5 oz.)
1 cup beef broth
1 bay leaf, crumbled
1/2 teaspoon garlic powder
1/4 teaspoon onion powder
1/2 teaspoon black pepper
1/2 teaspoon celery seeds
1/4 teaspoon paprika
1/2 cup slivered almonds

Boil the 4 cups of water and pour over wild rice. Let stand 30 minutes. Drain and place rice in casserole. Sauté onions and celery in margarine until transparent. Add to rice. Add mushrooms, soups, beef broth and spices; mix well. Top with almonds. Bake at 350 degrees F for 1 1/2 hours, covered. Add additional beef broth as needed. Yield: Serves 6.

Nutrition Facts

Serving Size 436 g

Amount Per Serving

Calories 284	Calories from Fat 127
	% Daily Value*
Total Fat 14.2g	**22%**
Saturated Fat 2.5g	**13%**
Trans Fat 0.0g	
Cholesterol 4mg	**1%**
Sodium 836mg	**35%**
Total Carbohydrates 31.8g	**11%**
Dietary Fiber 3.4g	**14%**
Sugars 3.4g	
Protein 9.5g	
Vitamin A 8% •	Vitamin C 4%
Calcium 6% •	Iron 16%

Nutrition Grade B+

* Based on a 2000 calorie diet

Spinach and Orange Salad

1 pkg. fresh spinach, washed & stemmed
Red onion, sliced thinly
2 cans mandarin oranges, drained (11 oz. each)

Dressing:
1/2 cup sugar
1 teaspoon salt
1 teaspoon dry mustard
3 tablespoons grated onion
1/3 cup vinegar
1 cup olive oil
2 teaspoons celery seed

Make salad by combining the spinach, onion and oranges. Combine sugar, salt, mustard, onion and vinegar in blender. Blend slowly. Switch blender to high and slowly pour in oil. Then add celery seed. Yield: Makes 1 1/2 cups of dressing or 12 servings.

NUTRITION FACTS PER SERVING: (BASED ON 2 TABLESPOONS DRESSING PER SERVING)

Nutrition Facts

Serving Size 121 g

Amount Per Serving

Calories 227	Calories from Fat 154
	% Daily Value*
Total Fat 17.1g	26%
Saturated Fat 2.4g	12%
Trans Fat 0.0g	
Cholesterol 0mg	0%
Sodium 218mg	9%
Total Carbohydrates 19.3g	6%
Dietary Fiber 1.3g	5%
Sugars 17.2g	
Protein 0.9g	

Vitamin A 48%	Vitamin C 33%
Calcium 5%	Iron 5%

Nutrition Grade C+
* Based on a 2000 calorie diet

Cauliflower Patties

1 head of cauliflower
1 egg
1/4 cup flour
1/8 teaspoon salt
1/8 teaspoon pepper
1/4 cup flour
1/2 cup vegetable oil

Remove flowerettes from head of cauliflower. Wash and cook covered with water until tender. Drain and mash. Add egg and salt and pepper. Add enough flour so patty holds its shape when spooned onto a hot griddle. Make 2" patties. Add oil to cover the bottom of a frying pan. Heat the oil until hot, then fry the patties on both sides until golden brown. Drain on paper towels. Yield: 12 patties, serves 4.

Nutrition Facts

Serving Size 120 g

Amount Per Serving

Calories 330	Calories from Fat 257
	% Daily Value*
Total Fat 28.6g	44%
Saturated Fat 5.7g	29%
Cholesterol 41mg	14%
Sodium 109mg	5%
Total Carbohydrates 15.6g	5%
Dietary Fiber 2.1g	8%
Sugars 1.7g	
Protein 4.3g	

Vitamin A 1%	Vitamin C 51%
Calcium 2%	Iron 7%

Nutrition Grade C
* Based on a 2000 calorie diet

Apricot Salad

1 can apricots, drained and quartered, reserve juice (17 oz.)
1 bottle maraschino cherries, halved, reserve juice (4 oz.)
1/4 cup cider vinegar
3 sticks cinnamon
1 tablespoon whole cloves
1 package lemon gelatin (3 oz.)
1 cup nuts, chopped

In a microwave-safe bowl, add enough water with apricot and cherry juice and vinegar to make 2 cups liquid. Add cinnamon sticks and cloves. Microwave on high 3 minutes and then turn to 50% power for 7 minutes. Cover and let sit several minutes. Remove cinnamon sticks and cloves. Add gelatin and stir until dissolved. Add apricots, cherries and nuts. Pour into mold or serving bowl. Chill. Yield: 4 servings.

Nutrition Facts

Serving Size 221 g

Amount Per Serving

Calories 426	Calories from Fat 162
	% Daily Value*
Total Fat 18.0g	28%
Saturated Fat 2.4g	12%
Trans Fat 0.0g	
Cholesterol 0mg	0%
Sodium 310mg	13%
Total Carbohydrates 60.5g	20%
Dietary Fiber 5.7g	23%
Sugars 44.5g	
Protein 7.7g	

Vitamin A 32%	Vitamin C 8%
Calcium 5%	Iron 11%

Nutrition Grade B
* Based on a 2000 calorie diet

Southern Spoon Bread

3/4 cup stone ground corn meal
1 1/2 teaspoons baking powder
1 teaspoon salt
1/2 teaspoon baking soda
3/4 cup boiling water
3 eggs
1 1/2 cups buttermilk
Nonstick cooking spray

Mix the corn meal, baking powder, salt and baking soda together. Gradually add boiling water, stirring constantly. Beat eggs until light and add to mixture. Stir in buttermilk and mix well. Generously spray a 1 1/2 to 2 quart casserole dish with cooking spray and pour the batter in the dish. Set casserole dish in a pan of water and bake at 400 degrees F for 45 minutes to 1 hour until bread is firm in the middle and top is golden. Yield: 6 generous servings.

Nutrition Facts

Serving Size 135 g

Amount Per Serving

Calories 123	Calories from Fat 30
	% Daily Value*
Total Fat 3.4g	5%
Saturated Fat 1.0g	5%
Trans Fat 0.0g	
Cholesterol 84mg	28%
Sodium 589mg	25%
Total Carbohydrates 18.3g	6%
Dietary Fiber 1.7g	7%
Sugars 3.1g	
Protein 6.4g	
Vitamin A 5%	Vitamin C 1%
Calcium 14%	Iron 6%

Nutrition Grade B
* Based on a 2000 calorie diet

California Vegetables

California medley frozen vegetables (20 oz.)
1 can green beans, drained (14.5 oz.)
1/2 lb. Velveeta® cheese, shredded
1 can cream of mushroom soup (10.5 oz.)
1/2 cup croutons
1/2 cup melted butter
Nonstick cooking spray

Mix the frozen vegetables and green beans in a 2 quart casserole dish sprayed with cooking spray. Mix in Velveeta® cheese and cream of mushroom soup. Sprinkle croutons on top. Pour melted butter over all. Bake at 350 degrees F for 30 minutes. Yield: 6 servings.

Nutrition Facts

Serving Size 272 g

Amount Per Serving

Calories 342	Calories from Fat 240
	% Daily Value*
Total Fat 26.6g	41%
Saturated Fat 15.2g	76%
Trans Fat 0.0g	
Cholesterol 68mg	23%
Sodium 1189mg	50%
Total Carbohydrates 17.1g	6%
Dietary Fiber 3.5g	14%
Sugars 6.8g	
Protein 10.3g	
Vitamin A 84%	Vitamin C 59%
Calcium 25%	Iron 10%

Nutrition Grade C
* Based on a 2000 calorie diet

German Potato Salad

6 medium potatoes
6 slices bacon
1 medium onion, sliced thin
2 tablespoons flour
3 tablespoons sugar
1 teaspoon celery seed
1 1/2 teaspoons salt
1/2 teaspoon pepper
3/4 cup water
1/4 to 1/3 cup vinegar

Microwave potatoes on high for 15 to 18 minutes and allow to stand wrapped in foil for 10 minutes. Cook bacon on high for 6 to 9 minutes or until crisp. Drain bacon, reserving 1/4 cup drippings. Place onion slices in dish with drippings and cook on high in microwave 2 to 3 minutes. Add flour, sugar, celery seed, salt and pepper, stirring to blend. Add water and vinegar. Cook on high in microwave 2 to 3 minutes. Peel and slice potatoes. Add to sauce and cook in microwave or on stove until hot. Crumble bacon and sprinkle over top. Serve hot. Yield: Serves 6.

Nutrition Facts

Serving Size 245 g

Amount Per Serving

Calories 210	Calories from Fat 26

	% Daily Value*
Total Fat 2.9g	5%
Saturated Fat 0.9g	5%
Trans Fat 0.0g	
Cholesterol 7mg	2%
Sodium 741mg	31%
Total Carbohydrates 40.1g	13%
Dietary Fiber 4.2g	17%
Sugars 8.4g	
Protein 6.3g	

Vitamin A 0%	•	Vitamin C	58%
Calcium 3%	•	Iron	10%

Nutrition Grade A-
* Based on a 2000 calorie diet

Ever-Ready Coleslaw

3/4 cup oil
1 cup sugar
1 cup cider vinegar
1 teaspoon mustard seeds
1 1/2 teaspoons celery seeds
1/2 teaspoon turmeric
1 teaspoon salt

Mix all ingredients above together in 1 quart microwavable dish and microwave 3 to 4 minutes on high or until mixture boils. Cool and pour over the following fixed vegetables:

1 medium cabbage, chopped
1 medium green pepper, chopped
1 medium onion, chopped
1 jar pimento, chopped (4 oz.)

Chill and serve. Yield: Serves 10.

Nutrition Facts

Serving Size 221 g

Amount Per Serving

Calories 268	Calories from Fat 150
	% Daily Value*
Total Fat 16.7g	**26%**
Saturated Fat 2.2g	**11%**
Trans Fat 0.1g	
Cholesterol 0mg	**0%**
Sodium 371mg	**15%**
Total Carbohydrates 29.0g	**10%**
Dietary Fiber 3.2g	**13%**
Sugars 25.0g	
Protein 1.9g	

Vitamin A 6%	•	Vitamin C 97%
Calcium 6%	•	Iron 5%

Nutrition Grade C+
* Based on a 2000 calorie diet

Fresh Spinach Salad

6 slices bacon
1 pound mushrooms, thinly sliced
1 pound spinach, washed
1/2 cup green onions, sliced
2 tablespoons olive oil
4 tablespoons lemon juice
2 tablespoons vinegar
1 cup sliced avocado
1 tomato, chopped

Microwave bacon 6 to 8 minutes on high. Remove bacon. Add onions to bacon fat. Microwave 1 to 2 minutes on high or until onions are soft. Add oil, lemon juice and vinegar to onion mixture. Pour over spinach, mushrooms, avocado and tomato. Toss in crumbled bacon. Serve at once. Yield: 4 servings.

Nutrition Facts

Serving Size 337 g

Amount Per Serving

Calories 233 — Calories from Fat 155

	% Daily Value*
Total Fat 17.2g	**26%**
Saturated Fat 3.3g	**16%**
Trans Fat 0.0g	
Cholesterol 10mg	**3%**
Sodium 324mg	**13%**
Total Carbohydrates 13.1g	**4%**
Dietary Fiber 6.7g	**27%**
Sugars 3.3g	
Protein 11.4g	

Vitamin A 216% • Vitamin C 80%
Calcium 13% • Iron 38%

Nutrition Grade A
* Based on a 2000 calorie diet

Rice Casserole

1 1/2 cups Minute Rice
2 tablespoons butter
3 cups broth
3/4 cup carrots, chopped or grated
3/4 cup celery, chopped
1 tablespoon parsley
1/2 cup onions, chopped

Heat the broth until it is hot. Brown rice in butter and add hot broth. Put in a 3 to 4 quart casserole, cover and bake at 350 degrees F for 35 minutes. Remove from oven and add vegetables, cover and bake for 15 minutes more. Yield: 4 servings.

Nutrition Facts

Serving Size 315 g

Amount Per Serving

Calories 351	Calories from Fat 66
	% Daily Value*
Total Fat 7.4g	**11%**
Saturated Fat 4.1g	**20%**
Trans Fat 0.0g	
Cholesterol 15mg	**5%**
Sodium 650mg	**27%**
Total Carbohydrates 60.2g	**20%**
Dietary Fiber 2.1g	**8%**
Sugars 2.6g	
Protein 9.2g	
Vitamin A 76%	Vitamin C 7%
Calcium 5%	Iron 20%

Nutrition Grade A-
* Based on a 2000 calorie diet

Carrot Casserole

4 cups cooked carrots
1/2 lb. Velveeta® cheese
1/3 cup melted margarine
2 tablespoons onion, chopped
1 cup Ritz crackers, crushed
Nonstick cooking spray

Spray casserole dish (9 x 12") with cooking spray. Layer carrots and cheese in dish. Pour margarine over carrots and cheese. Sprinkle onions over top and then sprinkle crushed crackers on top of that. Bake at 350 degrees F for 45 minutes. Yield: 4 servings.

Nutrition Facts

Serving Size 219 g

Amount Per Serving

Calories 495	Calories from Fat 323
	% Daily Value*
Total Fat 35.9g	**55%**
Saturated Fat 12.0g	**60%**
Trans Fat 0.0g	
Cholesterol 40mg	**13%**
Sodium 1257mg	**52%**
Total Carbohydrates 35.9g	**12%**
Dietary Fiber 3.2g	**13%**
Sugars 11.3g	
Protein 11.6g	

Vitamin A 376%	Vitamin C 11%
Calcium 38%	Iron 6%

Nutrition Grade C-
* Based on a 2000 calorie diet

Cheesy Hash Brown Potatoes

1 cup cheddar cheese
1 cup sour cream
1 lb. frozen hash browns, thawed
1/4 cup butter, melted
1/2 can cream of potato soup (10.5 oz.)
1 tablespoon onions
1/2 teaspoon salt
1/4 teaspoon pepper

Mix all ingredients together. Bake, uncovered, at 350 degrees F for one hour or until potatoes are tender. Yield: 8 servings.

Nutrition Facts

Serving Size 127 g

Amount Per Serving

Calories 331 — Calories from Fat 215

	% Daily Value*
Total Fat 23.9g	37%
Saturated Fat 11.6g	58%
Cholesterol 44mg	15%
Sodium 633mg	26%
Total Carbohydrates 23.2g	8%
Dietary Fiber 1.9g	8%
Sugars 1.3g	
Protein 6.5g	

Vitamin A 10% • Vitamin C 13%
Calcium 15% • Iron 3%

Nutrition Grade C+

* Based on a 2000 calorie diet

Nutritional Estimates

Nutritional information in this Fish and Game Cookbook is based on the USDA National Nutrition Database, last updated 12/14/2012. The nutritional estimates included in this cookbook provide information on the amount of calories, fat, saturated fat, cholesterol, sodium, carbohydrates, dietary fiber, sugar, and protein, as well as vitamins and minerals appearing in USDA Nutrition Database. Nutritional estimates are per serving.

This information is provided as a guide to choosing a healthy diet. The information is not intended for medical nutrition purposes. You should seek the advice of your physician or other qualified health provider with any questions you may have if you are following a strict diet for dietary or medical reasons.

The nutrition information listed here is based on standard recipes and product formulations; however, slight variations may occur due to use of an alternate ingredient, brand or differences in product assembly.

Other Books by Bonnie Scott

4 Ingredient Cookbook: 150 Quick & Easy Timesaving Recipes

Bacon Cookbook: 150 Easy Bacon Recipes

Slow Cooker Comfort Foods

150 Easy Classic Chicken Recipes

Grill It! 125 Easy Recipes

Soups, Sandwiches and Wraps

Simply Fleece

Cookie Indulgence: 150 Easy Cookie Recipes

Pies and Mini Pies

Holiday Recipes: 150 Easy Recipes and Gifts From Your Kitchen

CAMPING Books

100 Easy Camping Recipes

Camping Recipes: Foil Packet Cooking

IN JARS Books

100 Easy Recipes in Jars

100 More Easy Recipes in Jars

Desserts in Jars

All titles available in Paperback and Kindle versions at Amazon.com

Photo credits:
Thomas Harris/Photos.com, Cornstock Images, Dibas

Graphics by:
Dynamic Graphics

Made in United States
North Haven, CT
31 May 2024